Living Joyfully Free
Devotional - Volume 2

Continuing on the Joyful Journey

Lisa Buffaloe

Copyright @2014 Lisa Buffaloe
Published by John 15:11 Publications, Boise, ID

All rights reserved. No part of this book may be reproduced or transmitted in any way, form or by any means, electronic or mechanical—including photocopying, recording, or by any information storage and retrieval system—without permission of the publisher or the author. The only exception is brief quotations in printed reviews.

Scripture taken from the New Century Version® (NCV). Copyright © 2005 by Thomas Nelson, Inc. Used by permission. All rights reserved.
Scripture taken from the NEW AMERICAN STANDARD BIBLE® (NASB), Copyright © 1960, 1962, 1963 ,1968, 1971, 1972, 1973 ,1975, 1977, 1995 by The Lockman Foundation. Used by permission.
Scripture quotations marked (NLT) are taken from the Holy Bible, New Living Translation, copyright © 1996, 2004, 2007 by Tyndale House Foundation. Used by permission of Tyndale House Publishers, Inc., Carol Stream, Illinois 60188. All rights reserved.
THE HOLY BIBLE, NEW INTERNATIONAL VERSION®, NIV® Copyright © 1973, 1978, 1984, 2011 by Biblica, Inc.™ Used by permission. All rights reserved worldwide.
Scripture taken from the New King James Version®. Copyright © 1982 by Thomas Nelson, Inc. Used by permission. All rights reserved.
Scripture taken from *The Message*. Copyright © 1993, 1994, 1995, 1996, 2000, 2001, 2002. Used by permission of NavPress Publishing Group.
Scripture quotations marked HCSB are taken from the Holman Christian Standard Bible®, Copyright © 1999, 2000, 2002, 2003, 2009 by Holman Bible Publishers. Used by permission. Holman Christian Standard Bible®, Holman CSB®, and HCSB® are federally registered trademarks of Holman Bible Publishers. Scripture marked ERV, Copyright ©2006 World Bible Translation Center.

Cover Design: Scott Buffaloe, cover and interior photo: Lisa Buffaloe

ISBN: 978-0-9859295-7-2
ISBN: (Electronic) 978-0-9859295-8-9

~ Dedication ~

To Jesus Christ, my amazing Savior, thank You for Your grace, mercy, peace, and joy that blesses us with the ability in Living Joyfully Free!

~ *Welcome!* ~

Welcome to the second volume of Living Joyfully Free. I love to dig into God's truth, explore and mine through the treasures that fill the pages.

The Christian life is a pursuit of The One who pursues us, it is joy found in the glory beams of a morning sunset or buried in the rubble of life. Being a follower of Jesus is a stroll, run, sprint, dance, roller coaster ride, stomach-churning wild-ride that leads to eternal delight.

Living joyfully free is pressing into God's chest and listening to His heart. Like children we can come to our Heavenly Father and ask the hard questions, and yet live in wide-eyed wonder. Let's ponder and hold up God's truth to His light and watch the facets of His glory radiate.

My hope and prayer is that this book will take you deeper into God's love, because the more we understand and discover, the more we can live joyfully free. Thank you for joining me as the joyful journey continues.

~ Sickening Or Sweet ~

A beautiful flower, native to western Sumatra, stands nearly six feet tall, weighs thirty pounds, and the bloom is a deep purple measuring over four feet wide.

However, no one wants this plant growing in their yard. When the flower opens, the fragrance is compared to a mix of rotting vegetation and rotting flesh. The flower is aptly named the Corpse Plant. Hold the nose. Gag. Run for cover.

The summer before I left for college, I worked at a bank in the small town near our home. One guy was very nice. But the best thing about him was, no matter how hard he worked, even when he broke out in a sweat, he always smelled wonderful.

When he walked in the room, the oxygen level dropped as we tried to breathe in his clean fragrance. Decades later, the memory still makes me smile.

The way we walk and talk, our attitudes and our outlook, draw people to Christ or repel them. Can you imagine if Christians truly lived in ways to help a lost and hurting world lean close to Christ? Don't know about you, but I sure don't want to send anyone gagging or running for cover.

Our God is an amazing God – His grace, mercy, and love, pour into us through the salvation of Jesus Christ. No fragrance on earth could smell sweeter.

"God uses us to spread his knowledge everywhere like a sweet-smelling perfume. Our offering to God is this: We are the sweet smell of Christ among those who are being saved and among those who are being lost. To those who are lost, we are the smell of death that brings death, but to those who are being saved, we are the smell of life that brings life." ~ 2 Corinthians 2:14-16 (NCV)

~ Swinging Through The Jungle Of Life ~

"I am the vine; you are the branches. If a man remains in me and I in him, he will bear much fruit; apart from me you can do nothing." ~ John 15:5 (NIV)

The Buffaloe household understands living in the waiting mode. I battled Lyme disease and waited over eleven years for healing. For 448 days, my husband searched for work and interviewed around the country with many promising opportunities. We wondered at times if we weren't in the jungle swinging from vine to vine like Tarzan and Jane (complete with screams). Each time we let go of one "vine" we weren't sure there would be another to grab.

Isaiah 40:31 reminded us that those who wait on the Lord will renew their strength and mount up with wings like eagles. They will run and not be weary, walk and not be faint.

Waiting on a person or situation change depletes energy, but waiting on God grants renewal of strength. Viewpoint, isn't it? Not waiting on a jungle vine for rescue, but waiting on God.

Jesus says, *I am the vine; you are the branches. If a man remains in me and I in him, he will bear much fruit.* The key is waiting on God—The True Vine. The ever-growing, ever-nourishing, ever-providing, ever-loving, ever-faithful, ever-true, and ever-faithful Savior.

During that time of waiting, we grabbed hold of The True Vine who allowed us to soar on wings like eagles as we went swinging through life's jungle. And after 448 days (yes, I counted) of holding tight, God blessed us with a new job, a new state to call home, some tasty spiritual fruit, and deeper roots in His vine.

With God, we don't have to worry. We can't fall, we are grafted in and part of the True Vine. Yay!

Do you feel like you are swinging through the jungle of life? Review verses Deuteronomy 7:9, Psalm 145:13, 1 Corinthians 1:9, and 2 Thessalonians 3:3. Each one records God's faithfulness to His children.

List other verses that give you comfort during trials. Be assured and confident The True Vine will never let you fall.

~ *Praise Parachute* ~

Dragging my tail, I felt far from God, desperate for His touch. My sweet husband had searched for a job for eight months. School started for our son in twelve days, and our life remained stagnant in one big waiting and holding pattern.

A gentle voice nudged in my spirit, "Praise Me."

I'll be honest, I didn't jump right in. After a few minutes of hesitation, I turned on praise music. And as the songs played, I joined in the praise. Slowly at first. Hesitantly. And then as I allowed the music to wash over my weary soul, happy goose bumps popped on my arms and God's presence engulfed me.

And I wondered … are we made to praise? Do we need praise like we need sleep and to eat? Is that what feeds our soul?

Yes! To get through the problems of today, we are equipped with a safety device–*Praise*. Praise really does work. It's like a soul parachute that catches us as we fall and uplifts our soul.

I've pulled the praise rip cord many times during difficult seasons, and without fail I've received comfort and hope. Sometimes, praise brings a good, cleansing cry. Other times, gloom and doom are replaced with joy.

Praise provides reassurance as we nestle closer to God. Praise sends the demons of hell fleeing. And the best part — praise takes focus off the problems and back on our almighty, healing, gracious, compassionate, restoring God. For nothing is impossible for God.

Rough times bringing you down? Pull the praise rip cord!

Why are you downcast, O my soul? Why so disturbed within me? Put your hope in God, for I will yet praise Him, my Savior and my God. Praise be to the God and Father of our Lord Jesus Christ, the Father of compassion and the God of all comfort.

You have ordained praise because of your enemies, to silence the foe and the avenger. I will praise the Lord, who counsels me; even at night my heart instructs me. I call to the Lord, who is worthy of praise, and I am saved from my enemies. In God, whose word I praise, in God I trust; I will not be afraid. What can mortal man do to me?

Let the righteous rejoice in the Lord and take refuge in Him; let all the upright in heart praise Him! Let everything that has breath praise the Lord. Praise the Lord.
~ Psalm 41:11, 2 Corinthians 1:3, Psalm 8:2, Psalm 16:7, Psalm 18:3, Psalm 56:4, Psalm 64:10, Psalm 150:6.

~ Throwing Silverware ~

I've had some interesting dreams. Each one left me with points to ponder and lessons learned. Both dreams took place in medieval times.

The enemy was out there "somewhere" and our soldiers went out to search. I stayed behind, and while in the darkness, I saw the enemy's evil, bloody face. Without help and unarmed, I used the only thing available -- silverware.

Silverware?

I woke wondering ... where was my Sword of the Spirit, and why on earth did everyone split up?

Next dream – we are about to go to war, and we are moving forward as a group. My armor bearer delivers three pieces of armor. As I am reaching for them, two friends grab two pieces, and I'm left with only a breastplate. I'm promptly attacked by the enemy.

Again I woke frustrated, why was I not wearing my own armor, and where was my sword?

Does this sound familiar? As Christians are we standing firm together to battle the enemy? Are we battling ineffectively because we are using silverware (our own ideas or the world's methods) instead of our Sword of the Spirit (God's truth)?

Are we asking our friends to wear our armor (calling them for prayer and guidance instead of seeking God's wisdom), then wondering why we leave the battlefield defeated and bloody?

Heavenly Father I want to be ready at all times. Help me to put down the silverware, keep on my spiritual armor, and hold firmly to my Sword of the Spirit. Because in You and with You all battles are won.

~ Happy To Be Dead To Me ~

I locked gaze on the eyes looking back at me. "You are dead to me."

The face returned a smile.

With the feeling of freedom and complete joy, once more I said the words with gusto. "You are dead to me."

The face (my face) broke into a giggle, then a laugh, nodding with enthusiasm, prodding me to say it again. Once more I said the words, but this time added … "Not me, but Christ in me."

If I could high-five myself I would have. Woo hoo! Freedom!

I am longing to be dead to self, because when I get out of the way, God has more room inside of me.

When we rid ourselves of the tyranny of self, and the worry about self—who we are, how we live, where we live, what we do, job titles, and possessions, and our stuff—the more we live in the amazing freedom found in Christ.

Heavenly Father, I long to be dead to me so I may live fully in You. I want to walk in Your love, grace, mercy, and truth, free to be the best me I can be in You!

~ Lies Vs. Truth ~

The enemy lies, "You shouldn't have been born. You are a mistake."

God's Truth, ~ This is what the LORD says, who saved you, who formed you in your mother's body: I, the LORD, made everything, stretching out the skies by myself and spreading out the earth all alone. Before I made you in your mother's womb, I chose you. Before you were born, I set you apart for a special work. I say this because I know what I am planning for you. I have good plans for you, not plans to hurt you. I will give you hope and a good future. (see Isaiah 44:24, Jeremiah 1:5, Jeremiah 29:11).

The enemy lies, "No one loves or wants you."

God's Truth, ~ I have loved you with an everlasting love; I have drawn you to myself with loving-kindness. Jesus said, as the Father loved me, so have I loved you. For as high as the heavens are above the earth, so great is his steadfast love toward those who fear him. Long before he laid down earth's foundations, he had you in mind, had settled as the focus of his love, to be made whole and holy by his love. Long, long ago he decided to adopt us into his family through Jesus Christ. (What pleasure he took in planning this!) He wanted us to enter into the celebration of his lavish gift-giving by the hand of his beloved Son. It's in Christ we find out who we are and what we are living for. Long before we first heard of Christ and got our hopes up, he had his eye on us, had designs on us for glorious living, part of the overall purpose he is working out in everything and everyone (see Jeremiah 31:3, John 15:9, Psalm 103:11, Ephesians 1:3-6, Ephesians 11-12).

The enemy lies, "You are alone."

God's Truth, ~ Don't be afraid or discouraged, for the LORD will personally go ahead of you. He will be with you; He will neither fail you nor abandon you. Don't be afraid, for He is with you. Don't be discouraged, for He is your God. I will strengthen you and help you. I will hold you up with my victorious right hand. When you pass through the waters, I will be with you; and through the rivers, they shall not overwhelm you; when you walk through fire you shall not be burned, and the flame shall not consume you. For the LORD your God is living among you. He is a mighty savior. He will delight in you with gladness. With his love, he will calm all your fears. He will rejoice over you with joyful songs (see Deuteronomy 31:8, Isaiah 41:10, Isaiah 43:2, Zephaniah 3:17).

The enemy lies, "You've gone too far from God's grace."

God's Truth, ~ The LORD's power is enough to save you. He can hear you when you ask him for help. God's mercy is great, and he loves us very much. Though we were spiritually dead because of the things we did against God, he gave us new life with Christ. You have been saved by God's grace. And He raised us up with Christ and gave us a seat with Him in the heavens. He did this for those in Christ Jesus so for all future time he could show the very great riches of His grace by being kind to us in Christ Jesus. You've been saved by grace through believing. You didn't save yourselves; it was a gift from God. God rescued us from dead-end alleys and dark dungeons. He's set us up in the kingdom of Jesus who He loves so much, the Son who got us out of the pit we were in, got rid of the sins we were doomed to keep repeating (see Isaiah 59:1, Ephesians 2:4-8, Colossians 1:13-14).

The enemy lies, "No one understands you."

God's truth, ~ He knows when you sit down and when you get up. He knows your thoughts before you think them. He has compassion on you. He knows how you are formed and remembers we are but dust. He knows, understands and knows you (Psalm 139:2, Psalm 103:13-14, Jeremiah 9:24).

The enemy lies, "There is no hope or help."
God's truth, ~ Our help comes from the LORD, the Maker of heaven and earth. He won't let your foot slip. He watches over you and doesn't slumber or sleep. He's your shade at your right hand. The sun won't harm you by day, nor the moon by night. The Lord will keep you from all harm. He will watch over your life. He'll watch over your coming and going now and forever. The Lord is our help and our shield. Find rest my soul, in God alone. My hope comes from Him (see Psalm 33:20, Psalm 62:5, Psalm 121).

The enemy lies, "You are unprotected."
God's truth, ~ The name of the LORD is a strong tower, the righteous run to it and are safe. He is your hiding place. He will protect you from trouble and surround you with songs of deliverance. The Lord is faithful, and He will strengthen and protect you from the evil one. He will cover you with His feathers, and under His wings you will find refuge; His faithfulness will be your shield and rampart. He is your rock, fortress and deliverer. God is your rock, in whom you take refuge. He is your shield and stronghold (see Proverbs 18:10, Psalm 32:7, 2 Thessalonians 3:3, Psalm 91:4, Psalm 18:2).

You were formed and created by the God of the universe. In Christ, you are forgiven and free from condemnation, redeemed, restored, renewed, complete, and loved forever. And, that's the God-given truth! :)

Heavenly Father, no matter what I've been told, or what lies the enemy has planted in my head, help me to always remember Your truth.

~ Contemplating, Contemplations On Peace ~

I've been thinking about thinking, pondering about ponderings, and contemplating about contemplations. Life churns with turmoil—death, illness, joblessness, homelessness, murder, mayhem, economic woes, etc., etc., etc. With all these problems, how on earth do we keep from going stark raving mad?

Isaiah 26:3-4 in the Amplified version states that God ..."will guard him and keep him in perfect and constant peace whose mind (both its inclination and its character) is stayed on You, because he commits himself to You, leans on You, and hopes confidently in You. So trust in the Lord (commit yourself to Him, lean on Him, hope confidently in Him) forever; for the Lord God is an everlasting Rock."

Pretty cool, huh?

If I keep my thoughts on God, who He is, that He is in control, instead of worrying about today and what might happen, or what did happen, or the happenings of the hapless, I can be in "perfect and constant" peace. Oh man, does that sound great!

I love how The Message Bible puts Jesus' words in Matthew 11:28-30. "Are you tired? Worn out? Burned out on religion? Come to me. Get away with me and you'll recover your life. I'll show you how to take a real rest. Walk with me and work with me—watch how I do it. Learn the unforced rhythms of grace. I won't lay anything heavy or ill-fitting on you. Keep company with me and you'll learn to live freely and lightly."

I feel better already.

Want to contemplate with me on God's amazing peace?

Thank You Heavenly Father that we can contemplate You and in You we find the unforced rhythms of grace and perfect peace.

~ Tossed, Turned, And Tumbled ~

Ever find yourself in the middle of the night tossing and turning? The more you think, the more you keep thinking, and then your brain churns out impossible scenarios of monstrous proportions. Ack!

Fortunately, we do have weapons to combat this onslaught of onslaughting -- prayer, thankfulness, focus, and praise. A song of praise or a verse from God's word magnifies God and minimizes any problem or issue.

So next time you're up late at night, remember Paul's words… "Do not be anxious about anything, but in everything, by prayer and petition, with thanksgiving, present your requests to God. And the peace of God, which transcends all understanding, will guard your hearts and your minds in Christ Jesus. Finally, brothers, whatever is true, whatever is noble, whatever is right, whatever is pure, whatever is lovely, whatever is admirable—if anything is excellent or praiseworthy—think about such things. … And the God of peace will be with you. ~ Philippians 4:6-9 (NIV)

Heavenly Father, help me center my thoughts on You, changing my worries and fears to prayers, praise, and thankfulness. Thank You Father, that Your peace is never limited by our situations. Help me to place my concerns in Your capable, mighty, loving, and awesome Hands.

~ *Prayer Works* ~

Prayer doesn't change every situation and remove every hurt. Prayer doesn't always give us the answer we want. We can't see the big picture, and we don't know how the story ends, but we have a God who does.

Prayer lightens the weight of difficulties. Prayer readjusts the focus from our problems to our mighty, unfailing God. Prayer invites miracles. Prayer brings hope. Prayer prepares souls to receive God's message. Prayer tenders us to hear God's whispers in the midst of life's business or problems, heartaches, and pain.

Prayer ushers us into the presence of a God Who "by in consequence of the action of His power that is at work within us, is able to carry out His purpose and do superabundantly, far over and above all that we dare ask or think infinitely beyond our highest prayers, desires, thoughts, hopes, or dreams."*

Please remember to pray. God cares. God listens. And God knows best. Wrap your prayers in the knowledge you are loved exceedingly, abundantly more than you could ask or imagine. Talk to God, He's waiting to hear and longing to connect.

The prayer of a righteous man is powerful and effective. For the eyes of the Lord are on the righteous and His ears are attentive to their prayer.*

~ Ephesians 3:20 (AMP), James 5:16, 1 Peter 3:12

~ Stand Firm ~

What if what you pray for, long for, hope for, will only come through dark valleys?

James tells us to consider it all joy when you encounter various trials, knowing that the testing of your faith produces endurance. Let endurance have its perfect result, so you may be perfect and complete, lacking in nothing.*.

Will you abandon the cause, relinquish the fight, or turn away?

Jesus said, blessed are those who don't take offense at Him, who are not hindered from seeing the truth. We are given a living hope, reserved in heaven, protected by God's power. We can rejoice even during trials knowing that the testing of our faith results in praise, glory and honor at the revelation of Jesus Christ.*

Hard times are never wasted, and the things removed from our life are never without cause or purpose.

Because every branch in Jesus that bears fruit, He prunes it so it can bear more fruit.*

God's path is often difficult beyond imagination, because the easiest way is not the best way.

We need to remember to enter through the narrow gate; for the gate is wide and broad that leads to destruction.*

Your hearts desires (the desires for your loved ones), the deepest longings for fulfillment are only achieved through following God's path.

Delight yourself in the Lord and He will give you the desires of your heart. For He knows the plans He has for you, plans for welfare not for calamity to give you a future and a hope.*

The way is narrow and dark, but The Light of the world will always light The Way. Jesus said, 'I am the

Light of the world; he who follows Me will not walk in the darkness, but will have the Light of life.'*

Stand firm on God's truth. Be on alert, stand firm in the faith, be strong.*

Stand firm regardless of what life or the enemy throws your way. Put on the full armor of God, so you will be able to stand firm against the schemes of the devil, and having done everything, stand firm. Stand firm, having fastened on the belt of truth, and having put on the breastplate of righteousness.*

Stand firm to the end. For in the end, it will be worth it all.

"Behold, I stand at the door and knock; if anyone hears and listens to and heeds My voice and opens the door, I will come in to him and will eat with him, and he will eat with Me. He who overcomes (is victorious), I will grant him to sit beside Me on My throne, as I Myself overcame (was victorious) and sat down beside My Father on His throne." ~ Revelation 3:20-21 (AMP)

~ James 1:2-4, Matthew 11:6, 1, Peter 1:3-7, John 15:2, Matthew 7:13, Psalm 37:4, Jeremiah 29:11,. John 8:12, 1 Corinthians 16:13, Ephesians 6:11-14

~ Talk To Me ~

I visited on the phone with a precious friend, Natalie Nichols. Both of us suffered with Lyme's disease for years. She has me beat hands down on her journey though pain and difficulties, yet she is infused with the love of God.

I love the privilege of talking with my friends, whether in e-mail, phone calls, or in person. I love meeting new people and getting to know their stories. I miss them when I don't hear from them.

God wants to hear from us too. We were created for a relationship with Him. His Word tells us to pray without ceasing and to call on Him. He misses us when we don't call. I find it amazing and humbling that the God of the universe wants to hear from us.

As for me, I'm utterly, totally, completely, miserable when I don't stay in contact with God. At times I let the world keep me busy, and I wander away from His presence. But when I return, His arms are open wide and I crawl into His lap and let His love pour over me.

He's always waiting—all you have to do is call.

"Then you will call, and the LORD will answer; you will cry for help, and He will say: Here am I." ~ Isaiah 58:9 (NIV)

~ *What Did You Ask For Today?* ~

After a man passed away, his diary was found. Inside were more than twenty listings of specific mission stations in China. Notes indicated he had prayed fervently for revival in each location. After investigation they found God had indeed sent spiritual awakening to each place in the exact order this hidden intercessor had prayed. *

This quote by Dawson Troutman puts prayer in proper perspective, "Do you know why I often ask Christians, 'What's the biggest thing you've asked God for this week?' I remind them that they are going to God, the Father, the Maker of the Universe. The One who holds the world in His hands. What did you ask for? Did you ask for peanuts, toys, trinkets, or did you ask for continents?" ~ Dawson Troutman

"Ah, Sovereign LORD, you have made the heavens and the earth by your great power and outstretched arm. Nothing is too hard for you." ~ Jeremiah 32:17 (NIV)

*Wesley Duewel, Touch the World Through Prayer, Michigan: Zondervan, p176

~ A Message For You ~

God loves you. He really does. God's love is not like human love. There is no imperfection with God. God's love is pure and clean. God speaks through His Bible – His love letter to the world. His love is patient, kind, is not envious, does not boast, and is not proud.

God's love is not rude, is not self-seeking, is not easily angered, and through Jesus' grace keeps no record of wrongs. God's love does not delight in evil but rejoices with the truth. God's love always protects, always trusts, always hopes, and always perseveres. God's love never fails.

God is also a righteous and just God. Regardless of what happens here on earth, God's justice will be served. And with a righteous Judge the punishment always fits the crime.

God's love for you is not dependent on what you do for Him or how you perform. You have value because you are His beloved child. God, who created you, longs to communicate and spend time with you. You were created for fellowship.

God's thoughts for you outnumber the grains of sand, He sings over you while you sleep. You are so special to Him, He knows the number of hairs on your head, and your name is inscribed on the palms of His hands.

God's love reaches to the heavens, endures forever, is faithful, just, righteous, merciful, rich, abounding in love, great, everlasting to everlasting, gracious, and compassionate. The love of Christ is wide, long, high, and deep, a love that floods the soul with joy and unfailing love.

The richness of human love can't compare to God. His love is beyond the gentlest touch, the sweetest kiss, and the warmest embrace. Imagine the most tender love ever known, and multiply it by infinity and perhaps, just perhaps, you have a small glimpse of God's love.

And God's love, His amazing love, is available for you. He loves you.

Heavenly Father, thank You for Your amazing love. Thank You that You love us with an unfailing love. Help us to grasp the depth, width, and height of Your love. I love You, Father.

~ Loving With Christ's Love ~

Someone sent me a long message which hurt my feelings. I whimpered to my sweet hubby, prayed, and attempted to nurse my wounds.

Finally, after days of trying to come up with a response, I noticed she had sent the same message to someone else—it had nothing to do with me. I hung my head in shame when I realized I had forgotten to filter what I read through God and His love. Once I removed my pre-conceived notions, I was able to join her in her praise for God and His faithfulness.

It's easy to get hurt feelings and sometimes all the more so with our Christian family. Satan would love to make us angry and separate us from one another.

Jane Rubietta writes, "When I am loving others with Christ's love, I don't have to fear rejection or even being hurt by another. I am not the one being rejected—it is Christ. Nor do I have to fear depletion of that love as long as I'm resting and refilling... I am free to love passionately, to give joyfully, in spite of the possibility of pain in the offering, because it is Christ's love. And it is His love to which they will respond. Not mine. So when I love freely, live freely, then Christ is loving and living through me, and others see his beauty. God longs and intends to love others through the beauty of our loving."*

Father, please help me always give the grace You so freely give. Help me to hear what others say, and read what others write, with the filter of Your love. Help me to write, read, and speak with wisdom and love to uplift and encourage. Thank You, Father for the freedom that comes from You and through You. I love You Lord, help me to love always with the beauty of Your love.

*Grace Points: Growth and Guidance in Times of Change, Grayslake, IL: Abounding Publishing), p. 177. Copyright 2004 Jane Rubietta. Reprinted with permission of the author. Visit Jane at www.JaneRubietta.com

~ Comfort ~

"Praise be to the God and Father of our Lord Jesus Christ, the Father of compassion and the God of all comfort, who comforts us in all our troubles, so that we can comfort those in any trouble with the comfort we ourselves have received from God. For just as the sufferings of Christ flow over into our lives, so also through Christ our comfort overflows."
~ 2 Corinthians 1:3-5 (NIV)

Healing is an interesting process and seems to be a constant battle. Battles do leave scars and I've received my share.

What if our battles and scars were not just for us, but for others? What if what we went through (what we go through) is so we could tell others about God and His love? Oh my, it would so be worth every heartache, every tear, and every moment of pain, if I had the opportunity to share with others about God's wonderful love.

Life hurts and life is not fair, but God is fair and no matter what our battles, or scars, or how much we have suffered, God will right the wrongs, He will fight for us, and He will heal our wounds. I know because I see His touch every day even when I don't want to see, and even when I'm miserable. He doesn't give up and His love continues.

Call on God. He is faithful. He is the only one that is eternal, the only one that loves us with compassion and pure love.

Please take comfort knowing that living proof does exist, God can use those who have suffered. He can, and will, use those who have failures. The pages of the Bible are filled with people who were not perfect, but were used by God to accomplish mighty things for His Kingdom. They walked before us to remind us God doesn't require perfection. He provides perfection through His Son, Jesus Christ.

Jesus walked the dusty roads of this earth and experienced everything that we experience. He knows, understands, and cares. God, in the flesh of man, reached out to touch the sinner, the sick, and to heal the wounds of our fallen world.

Join me and reach out to the God of all comfort. He is safe. I know. He knows every ungodly thought and action I've ever done, and He still loves me. You can trust Him.

I'm praying for you. God is waiting. Come on in, there's room for all.

~ Grieving Heart ~

I've been grieving and mulling over grief. I was lied to, taken for a strange ride by someone I thought was a friend. I've made many connections over the Internet, and some of my friends own precious parts of my heart.

The risks are great to accept people at their word — to cry when they cry, to pray with them through times of hardships, and to lose sleep bringing them before God's throne.

My goal in writing and blogging is to point others to God, because I love Him. I love the changes God has made in my life. I love the healing He has done, and that He will walk with me through the highs and lows of my existence. I love and so appreciate that God knows the darkest parts of my heart and still continues to love me. I love His grace and mercy. I love that He restores and renews lives.

The Bible tells us that God's heart and spirit grieves. Why would God, who knows all things, willingly create people who will break His heart? Why didn't He squash me like a bug the times I walked away from Him? Why does He continue to reach out with grace and mercy?

Even through pain and heartache, God continues to love — because He is love.

And because God's love lives in me, I will continue to love, even when my heart aches. And I'll marvel, praise, and continue to tell others about the God who chooses to love even when His heart grieves.

"When we were unable to help ourselves, at the right time, Christ died for us, although we were living against God. Very few people will die to save the life of someone else. Although perhaps for a good person someone might possibly die. But God shows His great love for us in this way: Christ died for us while we were still sinners. The Lord says, 'I made myself known to people who were not looking for me. I was found by those who were not asking me for help. I said, 'Here I am. Here I am.'" ~ Romans 5:6-8 (NCV), Isaiah 65:1 (NCV)

~ Love Fertilizer ~

Spring's arrival finds us busy planting in our yard. I have never had such a tough time digging in soil (or lack thereof). Forget using anything bigger than a hand trowel since every millimeter is a hard fought battle through rocks, boulders, pebbles, stones, granite, clay, sand, more boulders, more rocks, more pebbles, more stones, and one ounce of dirt.

The weird thing is, we can remove forty-two zillion tons of rocks and our hole still isn't big enough to plant a baseball. I think if you pull out one pebble the others divide and multiply faster.

Needless to say, we added soil conditioner, starter fertilizer, Miracle Grow, planting soil, more planting soil, water, and lots of prayer.

Muscles aching we step back from each new addition, proud and grateful we have conquered and gained good ground. Without the proper ingredients our yard would only be useful as a stone quarry.

Yard work takes time and care, especially here in the high desert country of Idaho.

Relationships also take time and care. I'll be honest, I'm no expert on that, I have plenty of failures in my past. Thankfully, God's word gives us the perfect ingredients for healthy relationships.

So if we want a vibrant growing relationship we've got to get rid of the rocks/stones/pebbles—jealousy, being a braggart, haughtiness, rudeness, selfishness, impatience, and counting up the wrongs. Then replace with the good stuff/fertilizer/conditioner—patience, kindness, doesn't take pleasure in evil, rejoices in truth, accepting, always trusting, always hopeful, and ever-enduring.

Got rocky relationships? God is, and always has, the perfect miracle grow.

"Love is patient and kind. Love is not jealous, it does not brag, and it is not proud. Love is not rude, is not selfish, and does not get upset with others. Love does not count up wrongs that have been done. Love takes no pleasure in evil but rejoices over the truth. Love patiently accepts all things. It always trusts, always hopes, and always endures." ~ 1 Corinthians 13:4-7 (NCV)

~ Touch Of The Master's Hand ~

The story below is by a very special author.

"My wife is a very tender-hearted individual. Because of this nature, she adopted an animal left behind when others moved from what was now our home. The kitten had sought out a place of safety from the new feet going in and out of the house, the large truck, furniture being moved away, rooms emptied, until it became temporarily ignored and forgotten.

"By the time the move was completed a member of the family, not the one who usually cared for the animal, tried to catch it and place it in a pet carrier. The attempts were not well handled and the kitten became increasingly terrified. Subsequent return trips only reinforced the terror of the young animal.

"After we moved into the home, my wife began a personal crusade to show her affection for the alienated kitty. Slowly it began to respond, but at the sight of any strange feet (it's point of focus and sign of danger) it would run away to hide. In time the food and care did break down most of the barriers, but never all of them.

"This morning as I stopped to feed it, the cat disdained the food, but stayed close by, mewing softly, walking in circles, just a little beyond my offering. Then I stooped and reached forward my hand. In response, the cat moved slowly forward until it allowed my touch to come into contact with the velvety fur. The mewing turned to an instant purr.

"The need for food had not overcome its fear; it had been the response to love! And so it is with me—with us! We do not do the good that we should because we have to. We do things that frighten us, ignore the upset stomach, move past the trembling hands and the anxiety, to the touch of our Master's hand—the awareness of His pleasure in our offering; in response to an infilling of His love in our hearts. In finding the one who created us for Himself, we find ourselves. In finding His plan and daily leadership for our lives, we find the meaning for our lives. In paying the price for fulfilling those plans we find our peace." * ~ Jack Brewer

The transformation was amazing as the little kitty responded to the hands of love. It literally blossomed as the fur changed from coarse and stiff to soft and flowing. How do I know? The tenderhearted woman is my mother and the author of the story is my dad.

I have witnessed in people this same blossoming as they turned their lives to the Lord and responded to His touch. No matter the circumstances or the hardships, when the contact was made with their Savior, lives were never the same. The touch of the Master's hand is filled with love beyond imagination.

Heavenly Father thank You for Your touch that transforms and blossoms our lives in amazing ways. Touch my heart, soul, spirit, and mind with Your wonderful touch.

*Jack Brewer, Encounters of His Love, Unpublished, used by permission

~ On Fire With An Inextinguishable Flame ~

The following amazing story is true, only the name has been changed for protection.

As a young man Sahil* became involved with a gang and quickly became second in command. One night his mentor (the gang leader) was shot and killed, yet Sahil escaped harm and became the new "king," and sat on "his throne." Before too long he realized people would do anything he asked because they were afraid of him or wanted something from him. However there was no one who wanted to be around him just for him. Lacking any sense of intimacy or connection with any other person in his life – he desperately missed an intimate connection with someone – anyone.

Sahil's loneliness finally brought him to the point of desperation. He decided to take his own life. That night he lay down on his bed, ready to swallow rat poison he'd purchased. But just before he reached for it, he decided to call for help. He cried out to his Hindu gods asking them if they were real to speak to him and come to his aid. He gave them twenty minutes to respond.

No response. Total silence.

He decided to give them an extra five minutes grace-time.

Still, no response. Total silence.

Then he remembered a letter he'd received from his sponsor as a Compassion child. His sponsor signed his letters to Sahil with "Jesus loves you" and "God bless you." He decided to give this Jesus and the God of his sponsor a try. He cried out to God: "If you are real, you have five minutes to speak to me."

God spoke to Sahil.

He assured him He was the Truth.

Lisa Buffaloe 33

Sahil had now encountered God, and his life would never be the same. He gave his heart and his life to God. Sahil was so completely and radically transformed, the very next morning he knew exactly what he had to do. He went to the police station to confess all the crimes he'd committed and turned himself in.

The police weren't exactly sure what to do with Sahil. They weren't used to mobsters confessing and voluntarily turning themselves in. They sent him to the police commander. However, that police commander just happened to be a Christian. Upon hearing Sahil's story and seeing the amazing change in his life, all charges against him were dropped that day. Sahil was free to go. His slate – both in heaven and on earth – had been wiped clean.

Sahil told others about this amazing God that had so radically changed his life. Soon he became an evangelist/pastor/teacher, leading others to Christ and discipling them in the faith. Traveling from town to town, village to village, he shared the good news of the gospel of Jesus Christ.

At first, his techniques were rather unique. He explained, "When I was young and foolish, I would go into a village, pick up one of their Hindu gods, and smash it to the ground. Then I would say, 'See? I have smashed your god and nothing has happened to me. That's because my God is more powerful than this god.'"

In some villages, the villagers would listen. In others they didn't like the idea of their gods being smashed, and Sahil would be beaten. But that didn't stop him he'd just get up and head to the next village, ready to share the good news.

However in one particular village, they decided a simple beating would not be enough. They decided to set Sahil on fire. They tied him to a stake; stacked firewood all around him, then doused the firewood with kerosene.

However, the firewood wouldn't light.
So they doused the firewood with diesel fuel.
The fuel saturated firewood wouldn't light.
They decided to cover Sahil with diesel fuel.
He still wouldn't ignite.
Then, it started to rain...

The villagers realized perhaps they were dealing with something and Someone completely different. Not knowing exactly what to do, they decided to leave Sahil tied up overnight and try something else in the morning.

In the middle of the night, a young boy from the village came to Sahil and asked what he could do. Sahil asked to be untied. The boy did. The cover of darkness was perfect for Sahil's escape, however before leaving the village he stayed long enough to share the gospel with the young boy.

Several months later, Sahil was teaching a group of new pastors at a seminary-type gathering. A young man approached him, "I think I know you. Have you ever been in ------ village?"

"Yes, they tried to burn me at the stake there!" Sahil exclaimed. Then it dawned on him, the village that had once been completely opposed to the gospel, now had a young man at new preacher's training.

The young man told the most amazing story. After Sahil fled the village, the boy with which Sahil had shared the gospel, went home that night and told his parents all Sahil had said. The family believed the gospel was true, and gave their lives to Christ. Their lives became so radically different that the whole village noticed, and began to question the family wondering what had happened to make such a dramatic change. The family shared the gospel with the village. And the villagers came to Christ. And now, they'd sent this young man to learn how to be their new pastor.

Later Sahil sat on a train headed several hours away to a city where he was scheduled to preach. He wore his best preaching shirt. In his country a preaching shirt is one's best white shirt – beautifully and intricately embroidered. As he as sat on the train, enjoying the view, he suddenly heard God speak in his spirit. *Jump off the train, Sahil.*

Sahil just sat there thinking this couldn't really be God. Surely God wouldn't ask him to do something like that. Then again, the voice spoke. *Sahil, jump off the train.*

He argued in his spirit that he couldn't jump, it would ruin his best preaching shirt.

Yet God persisted. *Sahil, jump off the train.*

Sahil looked out the window. All he could see were rocks and steep drop-offs. It didn't make sense God would want him to jump off a moving train. *What about my preaching shirt, Lord?*

Sahil, jump off the train.

So Sahil did.

He thought when he opened his eyes he would see streets of gold. Instead all he could see was red mud – up to his chin. He'd landed right in the middle of a huge red mud puddle. His first reaction was anger that his best preaching shirt was dirty. It didn't even occur to him to be grateful that he was still alive; he was way too preoccupied about his ruined shirt.

Hearing a sound next to him, he turned to look. To his surprise, a man was in the same red puddle of mud only a few feet from Sahil.

That man had also jumped off the train.

"Sooooo, why'd you jump?" Sahil asked.

"I was trying to take my life." The man answered. "I thought when I jumped off the train, I'd fall on the rocks or down one of the cliffs."

Not missing an opportunity to evangelize, Sahil shared the gospel. And the man prayed to receive Christ right then and there.

Extracting themselves from the messy mud puddle, they walked toward the city where the train was headed. Coming across a pond, Sahil jumped in to wash and hopefully clean his shirt. But the washing didn't work; the red mud still remained. Even though he was frustrated with God, Sahil baptized the man. Afterwards, they journeyed on to the city discussing God as they walked.

Would you like to know what happened to that new believer?

The man became an effective and powerful evangelist, leading thousands to saving faith in Christ. Amazing what God will do to reach one soul, isn't it?

This God of ours – He is incredible. Sure makes the Christian life a wonderful adventure with an awesome God — even when we're muddy and mad.

Heavenly Father, thank You for men who burn with Your passion. Thank You that You use us even when we are so very human and can get angry at muddy preaching shirts. Use us for Your glory to tell others about Your amazing saving grace.

~ One Day ~

I wish I could save the world and stop the hurting. I wish I could be a mom for every mistreated child, and tuck them in safe at night. I wish evil didn't exist and everyone was nice.

But even with life's difficulties and heartaches, we do have a trustworthy God. His offer for everlasting life through His Son Jesus is true. God's promises are true, and His grace and mercy last forever.

We can believe and trust God because He is truth. God never contradicts Himself. When God says He loves with an unfailing love that is true. God's righteousness and holiness are true, and justice will be served. When God says He heals the brokenhearted and binds their wounds, He is speaking truth.

And one day all pain will be gone, and all tears tenderly wiped away, and we will be forever safe in God's love through infinity and beyond.

"Then I saw a new heaven and a new earth, for the first heaven and the first earth had passed away, and there was no longer any sea. I saw the Holy City, the new Jerusalem, coming down out of heaven from God, prepared as a bride beautifully dressed for her husband. And I heard a loud voice from the throne saying, 'Now the dwelling of God is with men, and he will live with them. They will be his people, and God himself will be with them and be their God. He will wipe every tear from their eyes. There will be no more death or mourning or crying or pain, for the old order of things has passed away.'" ~ Revelation 21:1-4 (NIV)

~ Never Wasted ~

My blog and websites are blessed by various visitors from around the world. Many are hurting and need prayer, and I am honored to carry their requests to God's throne.

Some people have been through horrific difficulties which drives me to tears and to my knees. I'll be honest; I so wish some of their journeys had not been true.

When hearing of suffering, it's easy to be overwhelmed or skeptical, but we all know people do horrible things to one another and illness and disease wreck havoc.

Without a doubt evil and pain exists, and prayer is needed to combat in the heavenly realms where war rages, for we do not only battle with flesh and blood.

Regardless of the circumstance or the request, we don't need to know all the details. Every need brought our way and delivered to God is filtered through His spirit to the one true God who knows all.

With God, prayers and tears are never wasted.

God is still in control, God is still bigger. God will right all wrongs, justice will be served, evil will be punished, health will be restored, lives renewed, and all tears tenderly wiped away. And until then, prayers and tears are never, ever wasted.

Heavenly Father thank You that Your word tells us that the righteous cry out, and You hear them; You deliver them from all their troubles. Evening, morning and noon we cry out in distress, and You hear our voices.

Thank You that You hear the needy and do not despise his captive people. Thank You that You are far from the wicked but You hear the prayer of the righteous. Help me to remember to pray continually. (Psalm 34:17,

Psalm 55:17, Psalm 69:33, Proverbs 15:29, 1 Thessalonians 5:17)

~ The Beauty Of Perspective ~

When we first moved to Idaho, our temporary living arrangement was an apartment on the third floor of a huge complex. If I opened our blinds, it seemed as though a thousand eyes could peer into the window. To the left of the kitchen table where I sat and typed on my laptop was a patio overlooking the parking lot. However, if you looked further you could see a beautiful mountain range.

No matter where I drive around town, I can see mountains providing a visual of Psalm 121, I lift up my eyes to the hills where does my help come from? My help comes from the LORD, the Maker of heaven and earth. He will not let your foot slip. He who watches over you will not slumber; indeed, He who watches over Israel will neither slumber nor sleep.

Regardless of our current situations, life here on earth is temporary, and Christ followers are guaranteed a happy ending. Our Heavenly Father provides the constant and consistent love and help we need.

When you look through the window of life, what do you see? Do you focus on the parking lot or do you notice the beauty of the mountains?

With the proper perspective filtered through God's lens, life truly is beautiful.

Thank You Father for this beautiful life. Help my perspective always to be through Your eyes.

~ Overwhelmed Or Overwhelming ~

Are you living overwhelmed or living with overwhelming victory? Overwhelming victory is ours through Christ (Romans 8:37).

Are you a conqueror? Remember we are more than conquerors through Jesus (Romans 8:37).

Do you know who you trust? I know the One in whom I trust, and I am sure He's able to guard what I've entrusted to him until the day of his return (2 Timothy 1:12).

Are you convinced? I am convinced God is able (2 Timothy 1:12).

Are you confident? I'm confident that God who started a good work in you will carry it to completion until the day of Christ Jesus (Philippians 1:6).

Are you persuaded? Abraham didn't waver in unbelief regarding the promise of God. He was strengthened in his faith and gave glory to God, being fully persuaded that God had power to do what He promised (Romans 4:20-21).

Are you living in triumph? Thank God, He leads us in Christ's triumphal procession (2 Corinthians 2:14).

Are you running to win? Everyone runs, but only one person gets the prize, so run to win! (1 Corinthians 9:24)

Are you convinced you are always safe in God's Hands? I'm convinced that nothing can ever separate us from God's love. Not death nor life, not angels or demons, not today's fears or worries about tomorrow—not even the power of hell can separate us from God's love (Romans 8:37-37).

Heavenly Father, even when life seems overwhelming, I want to live in Your overwhelming victory, fully trusting, convinced, confident, persuaded, living in triumph, running to win the race while forever safe in Your hands.

~ Scattering Seeds ~

Many days I begin by reading devotions written by bloggers, authors, speakers, and saints who now stand in the presence of the Lord. Their words encourage, uplift, leave me points to ponder, and verses to cherish.

Words spread across the continents through books, magazines, and newspapers. Approximately 153 million blogs exist on the internet. I sit at my computer and wish I could blog like Ann Voskamp, speak like Beth Moore, write deep theology like C.S. Lewis, and sing like ... well anyone who can actually sing.

However, I know I'm me. And the cool thing is, God doesn't make clones. We don't have to be like anyone else. God made me to be me, and you to be you. Your situation and circumstances bring unique perspectives.

We all scatter word seeds. Every word spoken, every letter written, can be for God's glory, tailor made for delivery, and tailor made for the receiver.

So my seed-sowing friends keep feeding on God's Word, so you may keep scattering worthy seeds.

"And God Who provides seed for the sower and bread for eating will also provide and multiply your resources for sowing and increase the fruits of your righteousness which manifests itself in active goodness, kindness, and charity." ~ 2 Corinthians 9:10 (AMP)

~ Counting Blessings ~

Have you ever awakened with anticipation for the new day? I did this morning. I have no earthly reason to be excited about today. There are no plans. But I do love mornings.

During the week, the Buffaloe household rises early. My sweet hubby's alarm goes off a little after five in the morning. I also attempt to get showered and dressed early. Once everyone is off to school and work, I have the house to myself. I can spend time with God, work on Bible study, e-mail, write, and read. Life is good.

I could be depressed; I have lots of valid excuses. There is a hymn which helps me get my perspective back on God, "Count your blessings, name them one by one. Count your blessings, see what God has done." And so I count my blessings. I want to be like our little dog. This morning he ran to the front windows shuddering with anticipation at the new day.

Even if the world around us is ripping apart at the seams, we have a God who loves with an unfailing love. We have a God bigger than any problem, worry, or concern.

For you who read this devotion this morning, I'm here at the cyber-window praying for you. I want you to know God loves you too. He is the God who provides for all our needs, He is the God of all comfort, peace, and joy. Filter your vision through Him, count your blessings, name them one by one, and see what God has done, and will do in your life.

Heavenly Father, satisfy us in the morning with Your unfailing love, that we may sing for joy and be glad all our days. (Psalm 90:14)

~ Re-New ~

Reflecting back, I've been pondering the bumpy road called life. I'm amazed at the remarkable things accomplished by God. Every turn and twist through this wild journey has led to a bevy of verbs beginning in "re".

Recounting God's goodness, I remember how He gives relief during times of difficulties bringing reprieves when most needed. Reflecting on those we have lost to death, yet rejoice that we will be reunited. God has retooled my thinking about trials as He renewed, restored, and repaired what the enemy meant for evil.

With reverence I marvel at rebirth through our Savior. When we repent, our lives are restored through the remission and removal of our sins. He refurbishes souls with His grace. God gently reminds us to refocus our thoughts on His greatness instead of our problems. He is our refuge and rescuer. With His help, we can resist Satan.

With God's touch, we can be revamped, recreated, rectified, redeemed, refined, refreshed, rehabilitated, reinvigorated, and no longer rejected. God's love, grace, and mercy remakes us, gently recreating us into the image of His wonderful Son. And in that truth, we can relax and rely in His hands, relishing the fact we are forever loved.

Heavenly Father thank You for Your amazing renewing, recreating touch!

~ Leaving Behind ~

With everything going on in the world, I started wondering … what would happen if I knew I had one month before the rapture?

Who would I tell about Jesus?

What would I want left in my house for someone to find?

Cars sometimes have bumper stickers warning they will be unmanned in case of rapture. What would they find in the seats or in the trunk? What is on the CD's, your MP3? What is playing on the radio?

If someone came in your house, what would be recorded on the TV? What is on the computer? What movies, books, magazines, and photos, would they find? What would they find in your drawers, closets, or under your bed?

Everything you leave behind will either turn someone away or point them to Jesus.

What would you leave behind to point someone to saving grace?

What are you leaving behind?

Remember to always be on the alert, for you don't know the day or the hour when I will return. (Matthew 25:13)

~ Note To Self ~

If self is dead, how would self know when self got self's feelings hurt?

If self walks away from flesh and walks in the Spirit, self walks in freedom.

If self relinquishes rights to self, self places self rights in The Right hands.

If self is not at peace, self should look to The One who is peace.

If self stops gazing at self, self can focus on God.

To be the best self, self must lay down self at the feet of self's Maker. For then self can truly live.

Do you need to give your self a note?

"You were taught, with regard to your former way of life, to put off your old self, which is being corrupted by its deceitful desires; to be made new in the attitude of your minds; and to put on the new self, created to be like God in true righteousness and holiness. What good is it for a man to gain the whole world, and yet lose or forfeit his very self?" ~ Ephesians 4:22-24, Luke 9:25 (NIV)

~ *Saying Goodbye* ~

I laid my head on Marlyn's bed rail, smelled the lotions and perfumes from those before who held the rail as they loved on her and said their goodbyes. The morphine drip and oxygen mask continued to run as she struggled for air. Her eyes were closed and her body limp, and still she breathed, her heart continued to pump.

We gathered around, touched her hair, her arms, and her hands. We whispered in her ear, told her we loved her. I hate cancer, hate disease, and hate to say goodbye. God can heal, and He does heal, because all around us are walking miracles. We prayed, read the Bible, and prayed again. Hoped, and begged God to please stretch out His hand and say, "Rise and walk." But the labored breaths continued, along with the sobs and cries of those who loved her.

I told my precious friend goodbye. Even if she didn't hear me, she knew I loved her. We didn't hold back feelings; you can't when someone is ill. But you shouldn't, even when they are not.

Don't wait to tell someone you love them or tell them they are special. I learned this lesson years ago when I stood by my best friend's bedside as she died from Leukemia. Don't wait. Right now call someone, send them an e-mail or drop a letter in the mailbox. Tell them you love them and you care.

I wanted God to heal Marlyn and take away her pain and cancer. But in the sorrow, I look for God. Life is hard, tragic, and unfair. But God is good. I still believe. Regardless of life's loss and hardships, I won't be persuaded to not believe.

I know God longs to comfort. I felt His touch as we gathered to say goodbye to our loved one. I saw God's sorrow in the tears. And I see God's love as He gathers His children into His tender arms to deliver them safely home.

Listen closely and you will hear their laughter. They will enjoy every moment, and will be waiting when it's our turn to come home.

Dear friend, the righteous are taken to be spared from evil. Do not fear, do not worry, your loved one rests peacefully with Me. ~ Your Loving Heavenly Father.

~ Emotional Cheese Grater ~

I felt like I had gone through an emotional cheese grater. As I wrote and edited a novel, I found myself in the midst of memories I had ignored or chose not to explore. I really didn't go willingly down that road. I went dragging and screaming.

God's gentle hands touched my heart, and He showed me there is nothing to fear. As I brought the past to His light, He took away the pain and hurt, and replaced with His healing touch.

Being a visual person, I need tangibles. So I wrote each incident and every situation on a piece of paper, prayed, and gave them all to God. I forgave those who hurt me. I also prayed forgiveness for my failures. When finished, I took the paper, set it on fire, and watched the smoke shrivel my past into oblivion. Now when the memories return, so does the picture embedded in my mind of the smoke and ashes as they drift toward heaven.

Trust Him wounded soul with your pain and your sorrow, for God is a God of restoration and resurrection. He can take the pieces of your painful past and again make them whole.

Heavenly Father You see trouble and grief. You take it in Your loving hand. The helpless put their trust in You for You are our help. (Psalm 10:14)

~ God's Masterpiece ~

No snowflake is created the same as another. Each individually formed ice crystal radiates sunlight as it flutter to the ground.

And you are a beautiful crystal of God's love, created unique for His unique purposes for a loving relationship. Regardless of age, body type, skin color, hair color (dyed or natural), rich or poor, you are all divine creations. You were created by love, for love, to love, created in the image of our glorious God.

You have value because you are His beloved child. Ephesians 2:10 says that you are God's masterpiece, created new in Christ Jesus so you can do the good things He planned for you.

You are God's purposeful masterpiece, doesn't that make you want to sit a little taller and walk with a bounce in your step?

And masterpieces have great value. Always remember, you are treasured by the God of the universe.

Heavenly Father, thank You. It's hard to believe I'm a masterpiece. I know all my faults, sins, and failures. How amazing that You also know them, provide mercy and forgiveness, and still love me. I can never thank You enough.

~ Believing To See ~

God's glory is often obvious, such as the flashes of lightning illuminating the sky or the thunder as it rumbles. Other times glory is found in unusual places -- a flower peeking through the crack on a city sidewalk or a smile from a stranger.

Sometimes glory is even found in the hardest difficulties of life. St. Augustine wrote, "In my deepest wound I saw Your glory and it dazzled me."

Everyone has been through difficulties. Some of you are traveling rough roads right now. It's so easy to focus on our problems. And some problems are humongous. We often forget we are made for eternity. This life here on earth is temporary; it's a mere blip on the radar screen of forever. And if we are in Christ, we always get the happy ending, and we truly do get to live happily ever after.

Jesus was good friends with a man, Lazarus, and his two sisters, Mary, and Martha. Lazarus became ill while Jesus was out of town. The sisters sent word for Him to come quickly. Jesus knew Lazarus was sick, knew he was dying, and yet Jesus waited to come. When He finally arrived, Lazarus had been dead four days. Martha ran to Jesus and said "If you had been here my brother wouldn't have died." That was true. Yet God had bigger plans.

Jesus told her, "Didn't I tell you if you believed you would see the glory of God."* And then Jesus called Lazarus from the tomb.

God's timing and God's ways are more than our earthly desires and limited vision can perceive or conceive. God has eternal purposes to display glory in amazing ways.

I was chewing on what Jesus said, and I wondered how often I don't see because I don't believe or I'm just not looking.

As I shopped at the grocery store, God was there as a little girl visited with a handicapped man. God was in that moment as they talked and laughed. Sweet fellowship. Sweet interaction. And in my spirit The Voice whispered, *"Did I not tell you if you believed you would see the glory of God?"*

When we believe, when we have eyes to see, ears to hear, and an open and willing spirit to God's ways and workings, we will see the glory of God.

Heavenly Father I want to see Your glory. I believe, help my unbelief. Help me to see You and how You are working in my life and in the world around me. I want to see Your glory!

~ Woe Is Me ~

Got the woes? Woe, woe, woe, your soul, roughly down the stream. Miserably, miserably, miserably, life is but a scream.

How often do we miss God's blessings? How often do we miss noticing how God is working, because we are so busy focusing on the woes? The negative woes on the news, the negative woes in our lives, the negative woes of our friends, spouses, children, and neighbors.

Woes woo us to watch their wanton, weaseling, wicked, wry, wrong, wretched workings. Woes make us whimper, whine, wince, and wilt.

Whoa on the woes! Let's whip the woes with the weighty wisdom of God's wonderful Word!

Heavenly Father help me to stop focusing on the negative woes of life, and look to the positives always positively found in You.

Why are you cast down my soul, and why are you in turmoil within me? Hope in God; for I will again praise Him, my salvation and my God. ... Jesus said 'If you abide in My word, you are truly My disciples, and you will know the truth, and the truth will set you free.'

So let's remember to think on whatever is true, whatever is honorable, whatever is just, whatever is pure, whatever is lovely, whatever is commendable, if there is any excellence, if there is anything worthy of praise, think about these things. (Psalm 42:5-6, John 8:31-32, Philippians 4:8)

~ Beauty Treatments ~

A glow stick is rather boring until it's broken and the chemicals mix and then glows from the inside. When we open our hearts to Jesus, He comes inside our hearts and His presence glows within.

And as we stay plugged into our power source by steeping ourselves in God's word and His presence, His glory continues to radiate from within us.

Did you realize God, His word, and Jesus are the ultimate beauty treatments? Moses face shone after spending time talking with God, so much so that he had to wear a veil over his face.

When we look to God our faces radiate with joy. If we live in God's love, we radiate God's love, because we radiate what is inside. We can glow with Christ. And we now reflect God's glory and are being transformed into ever-increasing glory. We aren't getting older, we are getting more glorious!

The Bible even talks about weight loss and weight gain. We are told our momentary affliction is preparing for us an eternal weight of glory beyond all comparison. Now that is one weight gain I don't mind!

And we are told to cast our burden on the Lord [releasing the weight of it] and He will sustain us. So friends let's cast off the burden weight, add on the glory, and gloriously radiate Christ!

Heavenly Father may Your Son glow brightly in me. Help me to drop any burden weight, and pick up the glory weight radiating Your love to the world!

~ Psalm 34:5, Exodus 34:29-35, 2 Corinthians 3:18, 2 Corinthians 4:17, Psalm 55:22.

~ Only One ~

"What man of you, having a hundred sheep, if he loses one of them, does not leave the ninety-nine in the wilderness, and go after the one which is lost until he finds it? And when he has found it, he lays it on his shoulders, rejoicing. And when he comes home, he calls together his friends and neighbors, saying to them, 'Rejoice with me, for I have found my sheep which was lost!'"~ Luke 15:4-6 (NKJV)

I'm so familiar with David, the shepherd boy turned King, that I often skim past his story. David was a shepherd, but not a complacent shepherd. He risked life and limb to rescue the sheep in his care.

And I wondered would I have taken on a bear or a lion to save one little lamb? To be honest, probably not—at least not without a bazooka.

Vicious predators didn't just turn and scamper away when David came to protect his flock. He had to grab those monsters by the hair and fight tooth and claw. And David was a just a kid. How can someone be that brave?

And then I think of Jesus who came to earth to snatch us from the teeth of our adversary. The Bible tells us the devil is a roaring lion looking for someone to devour. But Jesus Christ sacrificed His life to save us. No sin was too dark. No person too lost. Jesus came to save the whole world.

But even if the world only contained you – only one person … Jesus would have come to rescue you.

What thoughts come to your mind and heart when you reflect on the truth you are so valuable to Jesus that He would have come to save only you? Jesus loves you so much that He fought the enemy to save you. You are loved and never abandoned. Rejoice in His care.

Join me in thanking God for His unfailing love and His amazing rescue.

~ Kneeling On Tiptoed Knees ~

Early on Saturday mornings I meet with a group of women to pray. No agenda is given other than to pray as God's Spirit moves. We gather before God's throne, and I can't wait to see where God's Spirit will lead. Often we wait in silence, listening to God's Spirit and responding to the counsel of His Word.

Praise, thanksgiving, and scripture float as voices are filled with joy or weep for those lost, ill, or hurting. Our prayers have winged across continents to pray for the persecuted church and covered those needing healing, help, or salvation.

I visualize our group huddled together on knees before God's throne, bringing our spirits before our Abba, Father.

I feel so small. I'm a tiny girl, kneeling on tiptoed knees wanting, needing my Father's guidance, anticipating His presence.

How I desire every moment to live with open ears and heart. To unclench my hands to receive all He longs to give and my feet ready to venture wherever He leads.

And God meets us. His arms are always open, His ears attentive to His children's cry.

These precious moments. The God times. The absolute wonder and amazement of being able to come in His presence aren't limited to Saturday mornings or only for the elite.

Precious God times are open for all who seek. God promises… I love those who love Me, and those who seek Me find Me. You will seek Me and find Me when you seek Me with all your heart. (Proverbs 8:17, Jeremiah 29:13)

O that I would remember and my soul would stay knelt in God's presence, tiptoed in anticipation of His wonder.

Want to join me? Want to join Him?

Thank You Father that You love those who love You, and those who seek You find You. I'm kneeling in tiptoed knees at the wonder of You! (Proverbs 8:17)

~ What Will You Do With God's Son? ~

He came from Heaven above.

A gift of love. God born grace and mercy in the flesh of a man. Jesus, Son of God. Born to die, the ultimate sacrifice for man's sin. Crucified, died, and rose again. Nail-scarred hands offering forgiveness and eternal life. Jesus, Savior of the World.

What will you do with God's Son? Will you accept Him? Will you follow Him? Will you obey Him? Will you listen to Him? Will you love Him? Will you live your life for Him?

What will you do with God's Son?

When your time has ended on this earth and you stand in front of God, what will you answer when He asks, "What did you do with My Son?"

"For God so greatly loved and dearly prized the world that He [even] gave up His only begotten (unique) Son, so that whoever believes in (trusts in, clings to, relies on) Him shall not perish (come to destruction, be lost) but have eternal (everlasting) life." ~ John 3:16 (AMP)

~ Pockets Of His Heart ~

Sorrow surrounds me, and my long prayer list for family and friends brings me to tears. I am honored to pray for they have shared their pain, trials, and heartaches.

Several of my friends have incurable diseases and with horrific pain scream through the night. And yet they continue to honor and praise God, secure in the knowledge one day they will be cured, whether here or when they are safe in God's arms.

Other friends aren't so sure. Pain from the past has left scars inside and out. External wounds have healed, but the emotional pain remains.

I tuck their sorrow and pain into the pockets of my heart. I pray for their healing. I also pray for words to say and words to write, to show them that God's love is real.

Another friend shared something she never told anyone—except God. Afraid of being judged, her internal guilt and condemnation grew. When she told me, I cherished that she felt safe enough to share. I reassured her God forgives sins, and God would forgive her.

Because I continued to love her in spite of her failings, she accepted His truth. And I tucked her precious secret into my heart.

Messages, e-mails, and private conversations, shared details of sorrow and pain, keeping my heart tender and full. I carry their concerns to God. For each tear cried is precious, and God gently tucks them into His heart.

And one day when this life ends—and health is restored, justice is served, and sadness replaced with joy—we will be forever, enveloped safe in the pocket of His heart.

"You have taken account of my wanderings; Put my tears in Your bottle. Are they not in Your book?" ~ *Psalm 56:8 (NASB)*

~ Gifting Me ~

There are interesting and amazing contradictions and rebounds in God's kingdom — a right-side up thinking in a world turned upside down. A world that says look out for number one, store up riches, and the one with the most toys wins.

And yet God who created the universe, came in flesh and blood to offer Himself as a sacrifice for our sin. He Who gifted life, gifts again with abundant, eternal life through the nail-scarred hands of Jesus.

And we find in seeking God, God is found. In dying to self, eternal life is received. When offering ourselves to God, we receive more of God. Emptiness of me, results in an infilling of Him.

When giving cheerfully, God's blessings return, multiply, and continue eternally. In releasing all earthly riches to God, we obtain unfailing treasures. When making a positive difference in someone's life, we make a positive difference in ours. In blessing, we receive blessings.

Take me Heavenly Father, I gift me to You. Use me, I am Your child, Your willing vessel, empty me to be filled with You. Take my whole heart, my whole life, for my joy is forever found in You. I love You, Father. Forever and ever, Amen.

~ *Wilderness* ~

"Therefore, behold, I will allure her, will bring her into the wilderness, and speak comfort to her.~ Hosea 2:14 (NKJV)

Wilderness. Wild, lonely, barren. Wilderness — those times when friends don't call, the job is difficult or non-existent, provisions are scarce, the summers hot and the winters cold, the whole world doesn't seem to care or hear our cries and God seems so far away.

Yet in the wilderness, the distractions are removed. The still small voice can be heard, and that which is most important becomes clear. We see the God who sees us. God's glory, guidance, protection, and provision are found in the wilderness.

God allures us to the desert places to allow us to discover He is the only one who can fill our souls. God is the only One we need.

God is all we need.

Heavenly Father, thank You that our time in the wilderness is never wasted. Your plans and purposes are beyond our earthly reasoning, and Your ways are the best. Thank You for the times You draw us away so we can be drawn more deeply into Your heart.

~ No Buts ~

Every day we are asked questions.

How did you sleep?
How is your family?
How is your job?
How was your day?

How many times do we answer with a positive reply, but then add the "but"?

"I slept great, but I …"
"The family is fine, but …"
"I'm grateful for a job, but…"
"My day was good, but …."

I wonder how God feels when we say we are grateful, **but** we add a complaint.

Heavenly Father, thank You. Thank You for everything. Thank You for my life, my every breath, and all the provisions You bless me with every day. No buts about it, I'm so grateful. Thank You, Father. Thank You.

~ Toddler Fit ~

Ever have one of those days when you feel like you're running in circles screaming like a toddler? I've had several of those lately. Oh I so want to please God. I want to live in His perfect will. I want God to speak so clearly that I know what I should do with every moment.

Even during our Saturday morning prayer time, the mental image of me whining and running around in circles returned.

Then I read from Genesis 17:3, that Abram fell on his face, and God spoke to him. In that moment I saw my toddler self, falling on the floor, spent and sobbing. And my Heavenly Father gently picked me up knowing I was finally ready to hear what He had to say.

Can it really be that easy? Yes. Sweet surrender equals sweet communion.

Moses and Aaron fell facedown, and the glory of the Lord appeared to them (Numbers 20:6).

He bowed his head and fell on his face. And the Angel of the Lord said to him (Numbers 22:31-32).

I fell facedown, and I heard the voice of one speaking. (Ezekiel 1:28).

I fell on my face. Then the Spirit entered into me and set me on my feet; He spoke… (Ezekiel 3:23-24).

I fell upon my face and the Lord said to me. (Ezekiel 44:4).

They fell on their faces, Jesus came and touched them and said "Get up, and do not be afraid" (Matthew 17:6-7).

Heavenly Father, help me to stop fighting and running around in circles. Help me to fall into Your strong arms, because when I release me, I can hold on to You.

~ Storm Warning ~

Living in Texas we had grown somewhat accustomed to storms. The weather radar showed a line of thunderstorms moving across the state. Yet when friends called and asked if we wanted to join them for dinner at a local restaurant, we said yes.

While finishing dinner, we noticed the restaurant television showing the latest weather radar. The storm had increased speed, intensified, and a tornado was on the ground. We were directly in the path. We paid our bill and ran to our car, just as the first hail stones began to fall.

During the twenty minute drive home, we were hit with ice the size of golf balls and baseballs. My husband and I prayed for our safety and the safety of our teenage son who had remained home. Our cell phones wouldn't work, the car was pummeled mercilessly, and there was nowhere to pull over to find shelter.

By the time we arrived home, my poor husband was sore from head to toe from fighting to keep the car on the road, and our car looked like someone had attacked every inch with a hammer.

Our son and house were fine, and our car made it through the storm without major damage—a definite miracle given the size, intensity, and velocity of the hailstones. We did learn a valuable lesson. When they say the storms are coming—be prepared and don't ignore the warnings.

Trouble, temptation, and tribulation will come. Life won't always be filled with sunny skies. God promises to help us through every situation. He is our shelter in the storms. And someday Jesus will return to take home those who are His. We don't know when, but we are told to be prepared and ready. Don't wait. Don't take the chance. Don't ignore the warnings.

The storm warnings are here. Jesus is coming back. Are you ready?

Jesus will appear in the sky, and all nations of the earth will mourn. They will see the Son of Man coming on the clouds of the sky, with power and great glory. And He will send his angels with a loud trumpet call, and they will gather His elect from the four winds, from one end of the heavens to the other. No one knows the day or hour, not even the angels in heaven, nor the Son, but only the Father. I am coming soon! (Matthew 24:30-31,36, Revelation 22:12).

~ Soul CPR ~

My desk is littered with what looks like nuclear fallout from a paper bomb, 128 e-mail messages await reading, and documents are stacked on the floor by the shredder. To-do-lists sit next to my computer keyboard, laundry waits, and dishes are in the sink.

And inside, my soul churns from lack of Godly connection.

It's my own fault. I woke, had a quick quiet-time and hit the ground running. I have a tendency to want spiritual nutrition on the fly. Kind of like driving up to a gas pump, putting the hose in the tank, then speeding off after receiving a few drops. No wonder I'm puttering down life's highways.

Jesus tells us to seek first His Kingdom and His righteousness. When we focus on our problems more than we focus on God, overwhelming factors hit like tidal waves. However if we filter through God's hands each task and activity, there is a calming and a centering within our souls. We are promised grace for each moment, strength for every step, for nothing is impossible with God. Sounds all fine and dandy on paper, but much harder to practice.

Life is often like a tight-rope walk while juggling fifty-two tasks. I want to know everything will be good, everyone will be healthy, and money will be in the bank for today and tomorrow. I want assurance now, patience now, and happiness now, all while running through my day at top speed.

And in the quiet part of my soul God's whispers, *be still, cease striving, do not worry, I will provide all your needs, I will never leave or forsake you.*

I hesitate. Still not totally convinced, my feet keep moving, because somebody has to get all these things done.

The words from Psalm 23 float by in wind. *The Lord is my shepherd, I shall not be in want.*

But God, have you seen the checkbook balance? *He makes me lie down in green pastures. He leads me beside quiet waters.*

I visualize myself a sheep running through the pasture, splashing in the water, acting like a toddler fighting against nap time. *He restores my soul. He guides me in paths of righteousness for His name's sake.*

Restoration and guidance? Who has time for that? *Even though I walk through the valley of the shadow of death, I will fear no evil, for You are with me; Your rod and Your staff, they comfort me.*

Life gets scary, and I run back to God's arms looking for comfort. *You prepare a table before me in the presence of my enemies. You anoint my head with oil; my cup overflows.*

Settling in prayer and praise, I seat myself at His banquet table. All the issues, problems, and tasks slough off and clunk to the floor. *Surely goodness and mercy will follow me all the days of my life, and I will dwell in the house of the LORD forever.*

C – Connecting
P – Praising
R – Restoring

Happy, contented, sigh.

Thank You, Father.

~ Taking On The World ~

I love watching the Olympics. I'm so amazed at those who train and prepare their bodies to be the absolute best. During the Winter Olympics a television announcer commented that one particular Olympic athlete thrived on pressure. What if we had the same attitude when life gets difficult?

I started wondering how fun it would be to think of life as the Olympics. Just think, we are surrounded by a "great cloud of witnesses" rooting for us, holding up signs cheering us on. We could live each day as though it's a grand adventure, and hardship and trials, are merely methods for refinement and growth.

And at the end, for those who call Jesus Savior, there is always a prize – life everlasting, joy forever, and peace in God's presence.

After the Olympic competition the athlete was asked what was next in his life. His reply, "I don't know. Sleep, and then take on the world."

Sounds like a great plan. Woo hoo! Let's get some rest, rise up, and with Jesus take on the world!

Think of life as an Olympic event with a great cloud of witnesses, the angels, and friends and family who have gone before you, cheering you forward and Jesus by your side. What ways do your challenges take on a different light?

~ *The Ultimate Competition* ~

Being the only female in the house brings many opportunities to watch "manly" movies and television shows. Okay I'll admit, I do enjoy several of them. One is a Japanese television show, where competitors attempt to complete a punishing obstacle course which uses ever muscle group in the body.

I wouldn't make it past the starting gate.

People literally set up their own mini-courses at home and train for years. Each level of the competition becomes more difficult, and anyone who makes it through the first stage has my admiration.

Life is hard and often downright tough. Every day we face obstacles -- illness, death, job issues, parenting issues, children issues, people issues, life issues, issues with us, issues with issues … Argh!

However, what if we faced the day like athletes? The harder the difficulty, the more the honor, and the more prizes received at the finish line. When we keep our eyes on Jesus, we flex our faith muscles, learn more of who we are, discover more of God, and win our race.

So lace up those spiritual tennis shoes and compete to win!

To spiritually train for your life's race, read Hebrews 12:1-13. What verses apply most to your current situation? Remember, you are guaranteed to win when you're on Jesus' team!

~ Without Expectation ~

"Do not be afraid or discouraged, for the Lord will personally go ahead of you. He will be with you; He will neither fail you nor abandon you. For God is working in you, giving you the desire and the power to do what pleases Him." ~ Deuteronomy 31:8, Philippians 2:13 (NLT).

I've been a blogger and writer for years. I attended writer conferences and mentoring clinics, been blessed with a wonderful literary agent, and worked on honing my craft. I thought I knew where God was leading. Then last year, He opened a door to become a radio host. Me? Whimper.

After much prayer and God's assurance, I jumped into a new adventure. Equipment, software, and domain names were purchased for Living Joyfully Free Radio. A website was established, and I contacted people to be interviewed. No compensation is received. However the joy and blessings of sharing these wonderful testimonies about our amazing God are worth every moment of time, money, and effort.

Then God called me to step away from my sweet agent and go out into the publishing world on my own. More whimpering.

God's Spirit kept whispering into my soul that my journey would not be like the rest, but to keep my eyes on Him. However, I want to follow others and the typical pathways. I'm a Buffaloe. Shouldn't I be traveling in the herd?

So I hired editors to make sure my work is the best possible, and I published the stories God has blessed me to write. I'm still scared. But I want to be obedient. And not only obedient but live without expectations of what God will do on each of these adventures.

I'm still whimpering, but I want to please God above pleasing man. I want to live my life however God sees fit, to be used in whatever way He chooses. I'm clinging to God, His word, and His promises. And I'm living without expectations in the freedom and excitement of being and becoming who God wants me to be.

Heavenly Father, help me to live without expectations knowing that whatever You call me to do, will be the best.

~ Borrowing Grace ~

We want to borrow grace. We agonize over what others face, taking on their sufferings, imagining how we would feel in their situation. Sympathy and empathy are very important. However if we don't follow God's way, even if our intentions are good and honorable, we can find ourselves overburdened and weighted down, far too exhausted to have strength left to accomplish anything for ourselves or for others.

We want God to grant us grace for something that is not ours. God's grace is sufficient for every problem or difficulty we face. God's grace is sufficient for every problem or difficulty anyone faces.

There is a time to weep and mourn, a time to sit with friends, and let them cry on our shoulders. We are to pray for one another, encourage, help in ways that we can, but the burden is God's.

Jesus says in Matthew 11:30, that His yoke is easy and His burden is light.

Could we perhaps be picking up other people's burdens because we don't trust God will do what we think is right?

Can we trust God enough with our own burdens, and the burdens of others, to truly trust and rely on Him?

Our friends, our loved ones, those who walk through difficulties, need our prayers, need our help, but they don't need us to replace God.

Psalm 55:22 in The Message version, reminds us to "Pile your troubles on God's shoulders—he'll carry your load, he'll help you out. He'll never let good people topple into ruin."

Your worries, your concerns for yourself and others, pile them on to God's broad, loving, trustworthy, shoulders. He will carry every load.

"For with God nothing is ever impossible and no word from God shall be without power or impossible of fulfillment. My grace (My favor and loving-kindness and mercy) is enough." ~ Luke 1:37, 2 Corinthians 12:9 (AMP)

~ *Who Is God?* ~

Who is *your* God?

Is He God when He answers your prayers?
Is He God when He does your bidding?
Is He God when you get the job, house, car, or person you want?
Do you love God for what He *does* or *who He is*?
Is He God when your answers don't come?
Is He God when the answer is "no"?
Is He still God?

Is He still your God?

Oh Father God, You are my God forever and always.

~ Faith-Full ~

Are we Faith-"full" when we have enough money in the bank? When we and our family are healthy? When we are happy? When God answers our prayers the way we want them answered? When our stomachs are full? When we have enough possessions? When we get to do the things we want to do? When we have the job we want? When we have the family we want? When we can purchase the things we want? When life is good?

Is that *really* faith?

Now faith is the assurance (the confirmation, the title deed) of the things [we] hope for, being the proof of things [we] do not see and the conviction of their reality [faith perceiving as real fact what is not revealed to the senses]. Jesus said to the people who believed in him, 'You are truly my disciples if you remain faithful to my teachings. ~ Hebrews 11:1 (AMP), John 8:31 (NLT)

Are you faith"full"?

~ Night Watch ~

"My whole being shall be satisfied as with marrow and fatness; and my mouth shall praise You with joyful lips when I remember You upon my bed and meditate on You in the night watches. For You have been my help, and in the shadow of Your wings will I rejoice." ~ Psalm 63:5-7 (AMP)

At 2:44 a.m. I sit in my office wondering what God wants to say. The house is quiet. The world sleeps, and God has gently nudged me from slumber.

I miss so many of the opportunities He gives in the middle of the night. I roll over and return to sleep. Or I react in frustration and worry that if I stay up I'll be miserable during the day.

But then I remember The One who made me, will bless me with what I need in the way of rest. When He calls, He equips. So I sit with my hands perched on the keyboard and quietly wait. And in the stillness His presence brings a blanket of joy and love.

God wants to talk with us. He longs to sit and chat, and so often we are too busy during the day to stop. He lovingly calls in the night. And our souls wake.

And the time spent in the night watches will not sap us of strength, but infuse us with power from The One who is strength and power.

Tonight if you wake, talk to God. Time with Him will never be wasted. Rest in His presence, and mediate on His goodness. Dear friends, there is nothing more precious than spending precious time with God.

Heavenly Father, thank You for waking me tonight. Thank You for wanting to talk with me. I'm still amazed that the God of the universe wants to talk with each of us.

Help me not to miss a moment with You. Help me to remember that in Your presence is the fullness of joy (regardless of the hour). You made time, You made our bodies, and You promise to provide all we need. When we wake in the middle of the night, help us to enjoy the stillness of the moment and the time we can spend with You. Thank You for precious time in the night watches with You.

~ Snake Killin' ~

My dad found a small farm house on ten acres during my high school years and promptly moved us to the country. During our first month, my dad killed twelve poisonous snakes.

While us women-folk were home alone, a copperhead was spotted out front. Being the brave one, I retrieved my dad's 44 revolver and went out to do battle. The snake didn't move as I approached.

Standing only a few feet away, I aimed and fired. When the dust cleared, all that remained was a huge hole in the dirt. The snake, amazed at my idiocy or deafened by the boom, didn't move. My next shot didn't miss.

My dad became so adept at snake removal, the Blue-jays took notice. They literally flew to him, chirped to get his attention, then would lead him to where a snake was hiding. The snakes didn't have a chance. By the time my parents relocated, sixty three poisonous snakes had been killed.

Snake killin' needs to be part of life to remove those insidious, slithering, poisonous thoughts planted by the enemy. You know the ones – they tempt you to do wrong, or think badly about yourself and others, or try to keep everything in a negative filter.

Fortunately, God, our Heavenly Father, provides everything we need. The Message version of 2 Corinthians 10:5 puts it well, "We use our powerful God-tools for smashing warped philosophies, tearing down barriers erected against the truth of God, fitting every loose thought and emotion and impulse into the structure of life shaped by Christ. Our tools are ready at hand for clearing the ground of every obstruction and building lives of obedience into maturity."

Grab the heavenly ammunition, and let's keep our minds clear and our thoughts pure. There's snake killin' to be done!

Heavenly Father, thank You that nothing is too big for You. No nasty snakes or enemy attacks can stand against Your truth, might, and power. Help me never to shy away when there's snake killin' to be done.

~ *Looking For Hope* ~

Along life's journey we hope for certain things—good things for ourselves, our family, and our friends. However life doesn't always turn out like we planned and our hopes are sometimes shattered and fractured. We spend our lives looking for hope.

And often we focus so hard and so long at that one thing, that one person, that one situation, that we miss everything else. We miss the things God is doing, the people He is sending our way, the situations He is orchestrating to help us grow closer to Him.

People will fail us, circumstances are ever-changing, but the one constant is God. He is hope that never fails.

God's word helps us find His hopeful truth.

"Why am I so sad? Why am I so upset? I should put my hope in God and keep praising Him, my Savior and my God. Lead me by Your truth and teach me, for You are the God who saves me. All day long I put my hope in You. Let Your unfailing love surround us, LORD, for our hope is in You alone.

"Wait and hope for and expect the Lord; be brave and of good courage and let your heart be stout and enduring. Yes, wait for and hope for and expect the Lord. So be strong and courageous, all you who put your hope in the LORD! The Lord looks after those who fear him, those who put their hope in his love.

"And so, Lord, where do I put my hope? My only hope is in you. I find rest in God; only He gives me hope. You are my refuge and my shield; Your word is my source of hope. I am counting on the LORD; yes, I am counting on him. I have put my hope in His word.

"Those who wait for the Lord [who expect, look for, and hope in Him] shall change and renew their strength and power; they shall lift their wings and mount up [close to God] as eagles [mount up to the sun]; they shall run and not be weary, they shall walk and not faint or become tired. For I know the plans I have for you, says the LORD. They are plans for good and not for disaster, to give you a future and a hope."

Heavenly Father thank You that You are hope. We find hope in You, through You, by You, and can always know Your hope never fails.

~ Psalm 42:5 NCV, Psalm 25:5 NLT, Psalm 33:22 NLT, Psalm 27:14 AMP, Psalm 31:24 NLT, Psalm 33:18 NCV, Psalm 39:7 NLT, Psalm 62:5 NCV, Psalm 119:114 NLT, Psalm 130:5 NLT, Isaiah 40:31 AMP, Jeremiah 29:11 NLT.

~ If You Are Feeling ... ~

If you are feeling hopeless, where did you place your hope?

Why are you downcast, O my soul? Why so disturbed within me? Put your hope in God, for I will yet praise him, my Savior and my God. May your unfailing love rest upon us, O LORD, even as we put our hope in You (Psalm 42:11, Psalm 33:22).

If you are feeling soul thirsty and hungry, where are you going to find your soul nourishment?

Jesus said, 'I am the bread of life. He who comes to me will never go hungry, and he who believes in me will never be thirsty. If anyone is thirsty, let him come to me and drink. Whoever believes in me, as the Scripture has said, streams of living water will flow from within him (John 6:35, 7:37-38).

If you are feeling empty, where are you looking to be filled?

For in Christ all the fullness of the Deity lives in bodily form, and you've been given fullness in Christ, who is the head over every power and authority. Blessed are those who hunger and thirst for righteousness, for they will be filled (Colossians 2:9-10 Matthew 5:6).

If you are feeling unloved, remember Who loves you forever.

Though the mountains be shaken and the hills be removed, yet My unfailing love for you will not be shaken nor My covenant of peace be removed, says the Lord who has compassion on you. I have loved you with an everlasting love; I have drawn you with loving-kindness. The eyes of the Lord are on those who fear Him, on those whose hope is in His unfailing love. God loves righteousness and justice; the earth is full of His unfailing love. For God so loved the world that He gave His one and only Son, that whoever believes in Him shall not perish but have eternal life (Isaiah 54:10, Jeremiah 31:3, Psalm 33:18, Psalm 33:5, John 3:16).

In Christ you are never without hope, soul nourished, always filled, and forever loved!

Heavenly Father thank You for Your hope, Your nourishment, Your filling, and Your unfailing love.

~ *Whatever Is Required* ~

The other day in my quiet time, I felt this question prompt my spirit ... *Will you allow God to do whatever is necessary to prepare you for what He has planned for you and your family?*

The question sat in my notebook waiting for my response, and I chewed for weeks on what I would answer. Part of me leaped for joy at the thought of being willing to go wherever God leads and doing whatever He requests. The less adventurous, cautious, fearful/earthly side, shrank away unsure what God might require.

And I imagine the Israelites who hesitated in fear and lost their opportunity to enter the Promised Land. They missed entering a land of abundance, peace, and prosperity and were relegated to forty years of desert wandering.

I don't want to hesitate at the edge of something amazing because I am unsure what the next step might involve. I don't want to miss God's best. My answer is Yes.

How would you answer the above question?

Heavenly Father, I say YES! Yes, to whatever You want me to do and wherever You want me to go. Yes, I trust You with my life and the lives of my family members. Yes, I trust You to lead through dark and light, through good and bad, through hardship and joy.

Yes, I trust You to do whatever is necessary to me to align with Your perfect plan. I love YOU, Father and trust You wherever You lead!

Consecrate yourselves, for tomorrow the Lord will do wonders among you. And the LORD will guide you continually and satisfy your desire in scorched places and make your bones strong; and you shall be like a watered garden, like a spring of water, whose waters do not fail. For I know the plans I have for you, declares the Lord, plans for welfare and not for evil, to give you a future and a hope (Joshua 3:5, Isaiah 58:11, Jeremiah 29:11)

~ Don't Miss The Opportunity ~

I so appreciate the honesty of the Bible. God didn't hide the fact the people He used were imperfect. We tend to think of little David battling huge Goliath, Gideon and his tiny army conquering against incredible odds, and Moses leading the Israelites out of captivity. We forget the failures and the downright messes of those whose stories are listed in the Bible.

Every person, except Jesus, had sin in their lives. Yet even those who had been murderers, thieves, prostitutes, liars, and abundance of unsavory sins, went on to be used by God in amazing ways. They weren't perfect, many of them were a mess, but they were willing to turn to God, open their hearts, and walk in His ways.

Christians often miss ministering because we keep wanting/hoping/praying to be perfect before we minister. The testimony of our messy lives being redeemed by a Great God is what allows the sinner to see God's grace and mercy in action. We aren't perfect, but we serve a perfect God.

Please tell others the good news about what God has done in your life. Point them to a perfect God who loves enough to work on our imperfections. Show them the God Who restores the broken, loves with an unfailing love, reaches out to those who are hurting, and has arms wide open to forgive.

Heavenly Father thank You that Your grace covers our sin. Thank You that we can tell others of Your forgiveness, redemption, and restoration. Don't let me miss an opportunity to share You!

~ Night Patrol ~

What if every Christian who woke in the middle of the night spent that time in prayer? Not only would we become night watchmen, we would be on prayer patrol.

In the still of the night, think of the amazing things that could happen. Think of the Godly angelic activities that would be bolstered. Our soul ears would be attentive to follow the Holy Spirit's leading in prayer.

We could mediate on God's goodness, His word, His love and care, and His unfailing devotion. Our hearts could sing praises thanking Him for the mercy and grace that grant us eternal life. Our souls patrolling, praising, meditating, and moving against the forces of evil.

Evil bastions would be broken. Strongholds would be shattered. God's angelic warriors unleashed to set captives free.

So tonight if you wake, be excited! You've been chosen as a member of God's night patrol.

"Bless the LORD, all servants of the LORD, who serve by night in the house of the LORD! They delight in the law of the LORD, meditating on it day and night. I praise the Lord because He advises me.

"Even at night, I feel His leading. I call to remembrance my song in the night; with my heart I meditate and my spirit searches diligently. It is good to tell of Your love in the morning and of Your loyalty at night.

"Lord, I remember You at night, and I will obey Your teachings. In the middle of the night, I get up to thank you because Your laws are right.

"My eyes anticipate the night watches, that I may meditate on Your word. O Lord, I stand continually by day on the watchtower, and I am stationed every night at my guard post.

"The Lord will command His loving-kindness in the daytime, and in the night His song shall be with me, a prayer to the God of my life." ~ Psalm 134:1 (NASB), Psalm 1:2 (NLT), Psalm 16:7 (NCV), Psalm 77:6 (AMP), Psalm 92:2 9NCV), Psalm 119:55, Psalm 119:62 (NCV), Psalm 119:148, Isaiah 21:8 (NASB), Psalm 42:8 (AMP).

~ Don't Be A Clay Pigeon ~

I've found there is great danger if I become fixed in my ways and thoughts of how I think life should be and that I can fly in my own power.

Because when I don't stay soft and pliable in The Hands of The Potter, I might as well be a clay pigeon used for the enemy's target practice.

Heavenly Father, I don't want to harden, sit on a shelf, or be flung to the enemy. Help me to submit to any molding necessary to make me useful for Your kingdom.

"O Lord, You are our Father; we are the clay, and You our Potter, and we all are the work of Your hand." ~ Isaiah 64:8 (AMP)

~ Rest Break ~

Sunday afternoon. Church and lunch has come and gone. I gather my Bible, Bible study, and my Kindle with words waiting to be read.

Small heater blowing warmth into the room, I curl into my recliner. My soul kneels at God's feet, prayers of thanksgiving echo and travel to heaven's throne.

There are so many blessings–small and large–they all speak of God's love. I don't want to slip from earth's existence to life everlasting without watching, accepting, and experiencing the gifts of His hand.

I don't want to limit His love and power. I don't want my human thoughts, ideals, and desires to stand in His way.

And so I rest.

Stilling my soul in the depth of quiet, opening my heart to hear His voice, my praise wings to His indwelt presence.

Precious Heavenly Father, may I always dwell in Your presence and love.

Take time, make time to rest in His love.

"He who dwells in the shelter of the Most High will rest in the shadow of the Almighty." ~ Psalm 91:1 (NIV)

~ What If You Knew? ~

What if you knew Jesus was coming back next month?
Would you live differently?
Would you worry less about life and your savings account?
Would you be more generous with your time and money?
Would your prayers be more fervent?
Would you love God more?
Would you truly obey God's commands?
Would you love God with your actions and your words?
Would you be more bold and tell others the good news?

Don't waste a moment. Time is short.
Tomorrow is not guaranteed.

Don't be like those who say ... If only I had known...

"Just as you can identify a tree by its fruit, so you can identify people by their actions. Not everyone who calls out to me, 'Lord! Lord!' will enter the Kingdom of Heaven. Only those who actually do the will of My Father in heaven will enter.

"On judgment day many will say to me, 'Lord! Lord! We prophesied in your name and cast out demons in your name and performed many miracles in your name.' But I will reply, 'I never knew you. Get away from me, you who break God's laws. Behold, I am coming soon! My reward is with Me, and I will give to everyone according to what he has done. Yes, I am coming soon. Amen. Come, Lord Jesus." ~ Matthew 7:20-23 (NLT), Revelation 22:12, 20.

~ Saints On Call ~

When we pray for others, we are interceding and standing in the gap. We aren't just praying, we are Saints On Call.

Don't ever think your prayers don't matter or make a difference. Keep praying, and don't ever discount the power of prayer. Even when we can't see with human eyes, the prayers of righteous people are powerful and effective. For the eyes of the Lord are on the righteous and his ears are attentive to their prayer.

I urge you to remember that requests, prayers, intercession and thanksgiving be made for everyone. God looked for a man who would build up the wall and stand before Him in the gap on behalf of the land so He would not have to destroy it, but He found none.

Will you be the one who stands in the gap?

Let's stand in prayer SOCking it to the enemy together as Saints on Call. Pray on my SOC friends!

Heavenly Father, I'm reporting for SOC duty. Help me to never limit what You want to accomplish in my life and through my prayers.

~ James 5:16, 1 Peter 3:12, 1 Timothy 2:1. Ezekiel 22:30

~ Linking Shields ~

In need of prayer, I sent a precious friend a request. Her immediate reply came back … "Linking my shield with yours in prayer."

What an awesome visual. When we pray for one another, we are linking our shields of faith to stand firm against the enemy.

And when we link shields with God, nothing is impossible!

Heavenly Father help me to put on the full armor of God so I will resist the enemy. I want to stand firm with the belt of truth, the breastplate of righteousness, and my feet fitted with Your gospel of peace.

My shield of faith will be linked firmly with my brothers and sisters in Christ so we may extinguish the flaming arrows from the evil one.

Thank You for the helmet of salvation and the sword of the Spirit. I'll stay on alert with prayers and petitions praying in Your Spirit knowing with You all things are possible.

~ Choosing The Glory ~

Many lives are currently in a holding pattern of the unknown. Change is inevitable. And most of us don't like change. Unless of course, God responds to the changes we request.

God's ways are higher and bigger than we can imagine. And so we have a choice. We can stand firm on God's promises and God's love, knowing His ways are the best. Or we can stagger under the weight of what could happen or might happen.

We choose life's view.

As the beauty of a sunrise is revealed, will we choose to focus on the dark clouds or on the glories of God's perfect plan?

"Look at the ravens. They don't plant or harvest or store food in barns, for God feeds them. And you are far more valuable to him than any birds! Can all your worries add a single moment to your life And if worry can't accomplish a little thing like that, what's the use of worrying over bigger things? Look at the lilies and how they grow. They don't work or make their clothing, yet Solomon in all his glory was not dressed as beautifully as they are. And if God cares so wonderfully for flowers that are here today and thrown into the fire tomorrow, he will certainly care for you. Why do you have so little faith?" ~ Luke 12:24-28 (NLT)

~ Beauty From Ashes ~

God creates beauty from ashes and blossoms new things. Stephanie Shott is living proof of God's redemption and beautiful restoration.

This is Stephanie's story in her own words.

"It was 1962. Abortion wasn't legal but it was still dangerously available in back alleys and dim rooms where women risked their lives to end the life within. Nineteen year old Faye was on what she planned to be her final date with her controlling and intimidating boyfriend. When she told him it was over, things became violent. Rejection wasn't something he was willing to accept and so his rage turned into a brutal rape.

"Faye's hopes to end a terribly bad relationship turned into the beginning of something much worse. For nine months she carried the constant reminder of that horrific event within her. It was me. I was the reminder. Not just an unplanned pregnancy but a woman's worst nightmare. My birth-mom was faced with the pressure to end the life that was conceived so violently. But she understood that a life is a life, regardless of how it began...that while there may be accidental parents there are no accidental people.

"I entered the world with no first name. Just "Baby Salvatore". But four days later I left the hospital as Stephanie Tyler in the arms of two wonderful parents who would forever more be known to me as *Mom* and *Dad*. I was blessed with two wonderful parents who loved me as their own, but from the age of 3 until about the age of 12 my concept of life and love became skewed and shattered as I was repeatedly molested and raped by two different people in my family. Beaten, abused and broken by those who I should have been able to trust. I was a messed up little girl who never really knew what it was like to be a little girl.

"My teen years were lived on the wild side. Sexual abuse has a tendency to not only steal a girl's innocence but leave her feeling worthless, unloved and unlovable ... and so, I was pregnant at seventeen. Then married and divorced and a single mom by the age of nineteen. Another quick marriage and divorce became part of my story, as I spent the next five years looking for love in all the wrong places. It was in 'all the wrong places' that I met my husband, Donald. He was the drummer in the band and our lifestyle was a reflection of the whole rock and roll band scene. Not a pretty picture. But then again, no picture is pretty without God in the middle of it.

"Sitting in my apartment one afternoon, I watched a televangelist share a message I had never really heard before. Or maybe I had, but this time it began to make sense. I wanted what he talked about. Salvation. Eternal life. A real relationship with Jesus. But I also wanted my life to remain mine. And so it did. Even though the tears were real, my surrender to the Lord was not. I cried, prayed and thought I was saved but my life remained my own and I remained unchanged.

"About two years later, at the age of 24 I was ready. Ready to surrender all I was for all Jesus is. I knew He was the only one who could save my wretched self, and this time, I was not only ready – but I was willing. Everything changed that sweet October day in 1987. My heart, my life, my passions and my pursuits. For the first time in my life I didn't have to prove my love to someone else – I just had to receive God's love for me. He loved me. Dirty. Broken. Unlovable. Insignificant. Me. And nothing would ever be the same.

"It's been such a wild ride serving my amazing Savior. Time after time, year after year, He's called me to do what I'm incapable of. He has given me the privilege of ministering to women of all ages from a variety of backgrounds. He's taken me from classrooms to conferences, from small group meetings to the mission field, from women's ministry events to founding The M.O.M. Initiative.

"I'm more amazed than anyone that He has called me to serve women in the Word and that He invites me to participate with what He is doing on this planet! As one who has been forgiven much … as one who knows what broken is and what unlovable feels like, my heart echoes the words of Corrie Ten Boom, 'There is no pit so deep, that God is not deeper still!'

"Today, I have the privilege of sharing my story at conferences, pro-life events and on television and radio interviews. Unfortunately, one out of six women have a similar story to tell. Some are still looking for healing and hope. I'm so thankful that God gives me the privilege of sharing that He truly does make beauty of ashes. He has taken this girl with a bad past and a bleak future and redeemed my life from the pit.

"I don't know what your pit looks like. I don't know what your ashes may be. But I know Jesus came to heal your broken heart and to set you free. Not just from your sin and your self, but from all that holds your heart captive and keeps you from becoming who God created you to be. He did that for me and I know He longs to do the same for you. Don't you just love the way He loves us!? I know I do!"

I have been so blessed to watch God work in Stephanie's life. If you would like to hear more of her testimony, you can listen to her interview on Living Joyfully Free Radio.

The enemy hoped to extinguish Stephanie's life in the ashes of his evil touch, but God created amazing beauty through the glory of His loving touch in Stephanie Shott.

"The Spirit of the Lord God is upon me, because the Lord has anointed me to bring good news to the afflicted; He has sent me to bind up the brokenhearted, to proclaim liberty to captives and freedom to prisoners; to proclaim the favorable year of the Lord and the day of vengeance of our God; to comfort all who mourn, to grant those who mourn in Zion, giving them a garland instead of ashes, the oil of gladness instead of mourning, the mantle of praise instead of a spirit of fainting. So they will be called oaks of righteousness, the planting of the Lord, that He may be glorified." ~ Isaiah 61: 1-3 (NASB)

Stephanie's testimony used by permission.
Visit Stephanie at
www.StephanieShott.com or www.themominitiative.com

~ Whispered Love ~

An online issue needed my attention; I jetted out of bed at five in the morning and raced to my computer. Needing God's wisdom, I prayed for help, and kept praying as I searched for answers through help screens and forums. And as I continued to beg God for help, His still small voice whispered in my soul reminding me, I hadn't even said good morning or told Him I loved Him.

My heart stopped. And I stopped.

I picked up my Bible and moved into the other room away from the computer, away from the busyness of life to spend time with Him.

And God was waiting. And the time was so very sweet.

Don't miss His call. Don't miss the opportunities to spend time with God. To whisper your love to The One who loves you so.

"My heart has heard you say, 'Come and talk with me.' And my heart responds, 'LORD, I am coming.'" ~ Psalm 27:8 (NLT)

~ Armor Check ~

As Christians, we are given armor to stand against our enemy. Problem is, I wonder how often we leave our defenses locked in the closet.

We have to do more than just be aware of the existence of the armor of God. Paul cites several action words to make sure we are protected.

Be strong in the Lord and in His mighty power. Put on the full armor of God so you can stand against the devil's schemes. Our struggle isn't against flesh and blood, but against the rulers, against the authorities, against the powers of this dark world and against the spiritual forces of evil in the heavenly realms.

Therefore put on the full armor of God, so when the day of evil comes, you will be able to stand your ground, and after you've done everything, to stand.

Stand firm then, with the belt of truth buckled around your waist, with the breastplate of righteousness in place, and with feet fitted with the readiness of the gospel of peace.

In addition, take up the shield of faith, which extinguishes all the flaming arrows of the evil one. Take the helmet of salvation and the sword of the Spirit, which is the word of God. And pray in the Spirit on all occasions with all kinds of prayers and requests.

Our adversary is active and prowls around like a roaring lion looking for someone to devour. Don't go out unprepared and for heaven's sake, wear your armor!

Heavenly Father help me to remember always to be properly clothed in You and Your truth, each day for spiritual battle.

~ Ephesians 6:10-18, 1 Peter 5:8.

~ Outer Limits ~

Are our hopes too small, our dreams shallow, and our prayers limited and confined by our earthly ideas?

Jesus said with God all things are possible, and everything is possible for him who believes (Matthew 19:26, Mark 9:23).

What if we truly believed?

How far to the outer limits could our prayers go if we truly believed in an all-possible, all-mighty God?

Heavenly Father, take me to the outer limits with You. Don't let me block You and how You want to work in my life or in my prayers.

~ Undernourished And Flat-Lining ~

The last several days my brain seemed to be mentally flat-lining with very little happening in the synapses, other than misfires and duds.

A quiet remained between me and the heavens. Curious more than anxious, scriptures were searched, time spent in prayer, and praise songs were sung. Yet life stayed in a silent, holding pattern.

This morning, I stayed in bed wondering and praying about this situation. The verses came to mind regarding Elijah, and how God allowed Elijah to rest and recover before his next journey and mission.

Jesus tells us His burden is easy and His yoke is light. God beckons us to be still and know that He is God, and that He will guide us to quiet peaceful places to rest in His presence.

My brain hasn't been very active. However, in my spirit much has been accomplished. Distance from God didn't exist, except in my undernourished soul.

Thank You, Father. Thank You for quiet times to recoup, rest, and rediscover the wonders of You. Help me always remember nothing I offer this world is of value, unless filtered through Your touch and love. I love You, Father.

~ 1 Kings 19, Matthew 11:28-29, Psalm 46, Psalm 23

~ Patched Vision ~

I've been struggling. Struggling with motives and where and how to focus my energies.

My writing journey began years ago when I felt God impress these verses on my heart ... "I will stand on my guard post and station myself on the rampart; and I will keep watch to see what He will speak to me, and how I may reply when I am reproved. Then the LORD answered me and said, Record the vision and inscribe it on tablets that the one who reads it may run. For the vision is yet for the appointed time; it hastens toward the goal and it will not fail though it tarries, wait for it; for it will certainly come, it will not delay." ~ Habakkuk 2:1-3 (NASB)

I'll be honest; I had allowed "stuff" to cloud my vision. My understanding remained, but my heart grew weak and unfocused.

A dear friend sent me a quote from Ken Gott, "The eye of the heart has been lazy. The eye of our understanding has been strong. With renewal, God put a patch over our understanding to force the eye of the heart to work and become stronger."

Eureka, an eye of the heart opener!

Heavenly Father help me not to allow anything to cloud my vision of You.

"I ask—ask the God of our Master, Jesus Christ, the God of glory—to make (us) intelligent and discerning in knowing him personally, (our) eyes focused and clear, so that (we) can see exactly what it is he is calling (us) to do, grasp the immensity of this glorious way of life he has for his followers, oh, the utter extravagance of his work in us who trust him—endless energy, boundless strength!" ~ Ephesians 1:17-19 (MSG)

~ Refocus The Focus ~

I'm at my computer almost every day. A news report stated for good eye health, every twenty minutes you should focus on something at least twenty feet away.

What if we stopped and did the same in our daily walk?

What if we paused and checked to make sure our focus was on God instead of the problems that glare at us all day long?

Life would be so much clearer and so much better if we refocused our focus and realigned our thoughts with thoughts of our wonderful God.

"Blessed are your eyes, because they see." ~ Matthew 13:16 (NASB)

~ Waiting, Whining, Wanting ~

During the ten months we waited for our Texas house to sell, I became quite adept at whining. During that time I pulled out my back, which added to the pain of already herniated neck disks. We lowered the house price on our Texas house several times and still had no buyers.

Our apartment was getting more claustrophobic by the moment. Our son was about to start his senior high school year. I was preparing to attend a conference, and my conference clothing remained in the Texas house.

Then my husband walked our little dog, and a Rottweiler attacked. Hubby received lacerations on his hand from the leash trying to protect our pup. And our little dog sustained a bite wound and was on antibiotics and pain pills. Argh!

I had quite the dialogue with God. I wanted to feel better. I wanted to fly back to see our Texas friends, close on our house, and get settled in Idaho. I wanted our son to be settled before the start of the school year. I wanted our pup to have a yard where he could be safe. I wanted to get our stuff and make my Buffaloe nest. Yes, I had a bad case of the wants.

I knew I shouldn't whine. My innumerable blessings far outweighed any minor difficulties. As a "good" Christian I tried to keep a stiff upper lip, smile, and say everything is fine.

In a spiritual sense, I'm always fine. No matter what is happening, God is still good and He's in control. If I get my focus back on God and His sufficiency, I don't have to worry about any of those issues.

I'll tell you, I'm so grateful for the Psalms. David didn't mince words; he was honest enough to tell God exactly how he felt. Yet regardless of David's situation, he turned his difficulties into praise.

Sounds like a very good plan, I'm going to praise!

Thank You Heavenly Father for allowing us the freedom to vent. Thank You for giving us Your Word where we may find solace. Thank You that You know our every need and want, and You promise to do exceedingly beyond more than we can ask or imagine. Thank You, Father for eternal hope. I praise and love you so much!

"Why are you downcast, O my soul? Why so disturbed within me? Put your hope in God, for I will yet praise him, my Savior and my God" ~ Psalm 43:5 (NIV)

~ Lung Burning Lies ~

A lung burning lie that says I'll never be well, settles like a heavy weight on my chest during a return of illness. The lie also plays during flashbacks from negative past memories reminding me that in the natural sense I'll never be whole.

I know those are lies. God is more powerful than any illness. The God who created the universe can renew any life. There is nothing that the enemy hasn't sought to destroy that God can't restore.

Still those moments exist when breath is caught in my throat, and I'm needy and small. My scars are faded yet remain; reminding me that life can be so hard and unfair. Decades ago, Jesus saved me, yet every moment of every day I need His presence to save me from despair and deceit from the enemy. I need His presence to calm the storms, wipe away the tears, and hold me close. I can't do this alone.

God's truth is found in His word, in the true-life stories of those in the Bible whose lives were redeemed and restored. God's truth is found in those around you who have walked through hard roads, yet found freedom in Christ. God's truth is power greater than any of the enemy's lung burning lies.

"The LORD himself goes before you and will be with you; he will never leave you nor forsake you. Do not be afraid; do not be discouraged." ~ Deuteronomy 31:8 (NIV)

~ Never Give Up ~

Never give up. Frustration is natural, but persistence is key. Persistence, patience, learning, growing, and use your time to grow in God's truth and His Word. Life is not a quick race; it's a marathon with obstacles. And each obstacle gives you the opportunity for further growth and maturing.

Keep your hand on the plow, Jesus said no one who puts his hand to the plow and looks back is fit for service in the kingdom of God (Luke 9:62).

Run the race to get a prize and to win (1 Corinthians 9:24).

Be diligent in the matters of God, give yourself wholly to them (1 Timothy 4:15).

Be diligent to present yourself approved to God as a workman, unashamed and accurately handling the word of truth (2 Timothy 2:15).

Abound in every good work, grow in the grace and knowledge of our Lord and Savior Jesus Christ (2 Peter 3:18).

Fight the good fight, take hold of eternal life (1 Timothy 6:12).

God is faithful to complete what He starts, so finish the work you've been called to do with eager willingness (2 Corinthians 8:11).

Keep going. Keep going, Keep going. God is with you. **Never give up**.

Heavenly Father I desire to do Your will, Your law is in my heart. I will praise You. All glory to You. Thank You that You equip us for everything to do Your will.

May I be pleasing to You, fervent in prayer and zeal to serve You. I will be joyful in hope, patient in affliction, and faithful in prayer. I will never give up loving You (Psalm 40:8, Psalm 54:6, Psalm 115:1, Hebrews 13:20-21, Romans 12:11-12, Psalm 116:1).

~ Tell Them ~

Tell them how God saved you.
Tell them what God has done for you.
Tell what God has done for others.
Tell your children, friends, family, those you know, and those you meet, about God.
Tell of God's wonderful grace.
Tell of God's bountiful mercy.
Tell of God's amazing love.

Even the heavens are telling of the glory of God.
(Psalm 19:1)

Will you tell?

I will give thanks to the LORD with all my heart; I will tell of all His wonders. Come and hear, all who fear God, And I will tell of what He has done for my soul. My mouth shall tell of His righteousness and of His salvation all day long.

As for me, the nearness of God is my good; I have made the Lord GOD my refuge that I may tell of all His works.

Tell to the generations to come the praises of the LORD, and His strength and His wondrous works that He has done. So that the generation to come might know, even the children yet to be born, that they may arise and tell them to their children.

So we God's people and the sheep of His pasture will give thanks to Him forever; to all generations we will tell of His praise.

Tell of His glory among the nations, His wonderful deeds among all the peoples. Men shall speak of the power of Your awesome acts, and I will tell of Your greatness. But we ourselves cannot help telling what we have seen and heard. Psalm 9:1, Psalm 66:16, Psalm 71:15, Psalm 73:28, Psalm 78:4, Psalm 78:6, Psalm 79:13, Psalm 96:3, Psalm 145:6, Acts 4:20)

~ Faith Walk In The Darkness ~

Okay, I'll be honest. I hurt. My body hurts. Pain is rampant. Fatigue attacks and clings like a dirty dishrag. My health hasn't been the best for weeks, and the pain has gotten worse. Two bad dreams set fear in motion of another attack. I'm scared. Trusting but scared.

The spiritual walk is an interesting one. It's a walk on water experience in the midst of horrible storms. It's reaching out to The One who can take away every infirmity, and trusting His healing will come. And trusting even when His healing doesn't come.

Faith is praying and believing even when the road is dark and the pathway is littered with obstacles and heartaches. My friend, Linda Stevens, shared in an e-mail, "Prayer for help through the darkness IS what faith is. If there was no darkness, it wouldn't be faith."

I have faith. I know God will take care of me. He always has. He always will. He never leaves us or forsakes us. His promise is good. His word is true. His word sustains, comforts, guides, and brings hope.

We don't always get instant answers, instant healing, and problem free days, but we always have God. No matter what you face, regardless how dark the pathway, God is with you.

Heavenly Father I'm walking in faith in the midst of the darkness, knowing that nothing is too dark for You because You are The light.

~ ALL ~

All is a great word!

I want it all. I want to give all. Do all. Live all. Submit all, with all I have to my all-encompassing, amazing God. Because in giving all, I gain ALL!

Let my tongue sing of Your word, For all Your commandments are righteousness. You are near, O LORD, and all Your commandments are truth. And you shall love the Lord Your God with all your heart, and with all your soul, and with all your mind, and with all your strength. Casting all your anxiety on Him, because He cares for you. Who pardons all your iniquities, Who heals all your diseases. For He will give His angels charge concerning you, to guard you in all your ways.

For this reason also, since the day we heard of it, we have not ceased to pray for you and to ask that you may be filled with the knowledge of His will in all spiritual wisdom and understanding, so that you will walk in a manner worthy of the Lord, to please Him in all respects.

Bearing fruit in every good work and increasing in the knowledge of God; strengthened with all power, according to His glorious might, for the attaining of all steadfastness and patience; joyously giving thanks to the Father, who has qualified us to share in the inheritance of the saints in Light.

For He rescued us from the domain of darkness, and transferred us to the kingdom of His beloved Son, in whom we have redemption, the forgiveness of sins. He is the image of the invisible God, the firstborn of all creation. For by Him all things were created, both in the heavens and on earth, visible and invisible, whether thrones or dominions or rulers or authorities—all things have been created through Him and for Him. He is before all things, and in Him all things hold together. He is also head of the body, the church; and He is the beginning, the firstborn from the dead, so that He Himself will come to have first place in everything. For it was the Father's good pleasure for all the fullness to dwell in Him, and through Him to reconcile all things to Himself, having made peace through the blood of His cross; through Him, I say, whether things on earth or things in heaven.

And we know that God causes all things to work together for good to those who love God, to those who are called according to His purpose. For I can do all things through Him who strengthens me. My God will supply all your needs according to His riches in glory in Christ Jesus. Do all things without grumbling or disputing. Whether you eat or drink, or whatever you do, do all to the glory of God. To the only God our Savior, through Jesus Christ our Lord, be glory, majesty, dominion and authority, before all time and now and forever. Amen.

Dear Heavenly Father, I give you my all!!

~ Psalm 119:172, Psalm 119:151, Mark 12:30, 1 Peter 5:7, Psalm 103:3, Psalm 91:11, Colossians 1:9-20, Romans 8:28, Philippians 4:13, 19, Philippians 2:14, 1 Corinthians 10:31, Jude 1:25 NASB.

~ Set Free ~

Jan Coates life could be a made-for-TV movie. Raised by a mentally ill mother, Jan endured a childhood filled with unthinkable physical, emotional, and sexual abuse. Consumed with shame and guilt, she found expression in destructive acts against herself and others. Jan writes, "I tried to fix everything on my own. I failed miserably."

By the time she was nineteen, she was divorced with a young son. In 1982 a drunk driver killed that son, her only birth child. This tragedy left her emotionally paralyzed and numb. Jan, completely broken and at the lowest point in her life, cried out to God.

Jan shares, "The Lord heard my cry and responded to me with his love, mercy, and grace. I'm living proof that it doesn't matter who we were yesterday, or what we did—it matters that God wants to do something with our lives today.

Throughout the ages, God continually chooses to heal and transform the most improbable candidates. Why? I believe because the Lord wants to make clear that the power lies in him, not in people. When people observe drastic change in broken lives, their eyes turn heavenward."

By God's grace, she overcame her childhood abuse, dysfunctional family relations, divorce, the loss of her only biological child, depression, cancer, and much more.

Now, as an international speaker, lay counselor, author, and consultant, Jan Coates ministers to countless individuals how they too can be set free. She is the founder of Set Free Today–a ministry designed to help release the past and pursue the future.

Set free by our Awesome God, Jan Coates continues to help others find freedom and healing in Christ.

Heavenly Father thank You for Your amazing freedom and healing. Thank You that no life is too messed up to be set free by Your loving touch.

Jan's story is used by permission. You can listen to more of Jan's testimony on Living Joyfully Free Radio (www.livingjoyfullyfree.com) or visit Jan at her websites, www.JanCoates.com, or www.SetFreeToday.com

~ Truth For Tough Times ~

God provides comfort. His promises preserve our lives. His unfailing love is our comfort. His laws provide comfort (Psalm119:50, Psalm 119:76, Psalm 119:52).

God provides strength. The Lord is the everlasting God, the creator. He doesn't grow tired or weary; His understanding is beyond what we can fathom. He gives strength to the weary and increases the power of the weak. Those who hope in the Lord will renew their strength. They will soar on eagle wings, running and not growing weary, walking and not fainting. God is the strength of my heart. It is God who arms me with strength (Isaiah 40:28-31, Psalm 73:26, Psalm 18:32).

God provides rest. Jesus said come to Me and I will give you rest. Be still and rest in the Lord. Be still and know that He is God, He makes me lie down and restores my soul (Matthew 11:28-29, Psalm 37:7, Psalm 46:10, Psalm 23:2-3).

God protects us from fear. When I am afraid, I will trust in God, whose word I praise, in God I trust; I will not be afraid. Be strong and courageous. Do not be terrified; do not be discouraged, for the LORD your God will be with you wherever you go. God is my strength and shield. My heart trusts in Him and I am helped. The Lord is the strength of His people. God is our refuge and strength, ever present help in trouble (Psalm 56:3-4, Joshua 1:9, Psalm 28:7-8, Psalm 46:1).

God's hope never fails. The eyes of the LORD are on those who fear Him, on those whose hope is in His unfailing love. No one who hopes in You will ever be put to shame. My hope is in You all day long. Be strong and take heart, all you who hope in the Lord. Find rest my soul in God alone; my hope comes from Him (Psalm 33:18, Psalm 25:3, Psalm 25:5, Psalm 31:24, Psalm 62:5).

Thank You Father, for verses that flow freely from Your word to give us hope, comfort, and strength. Thank You that even in suffering we can rejoice, knowing that suffering produces perseverance; perseverance, character; and character, hope. And hope never disappoints because You God have poured Your love into our hearts through Your Holy Spirit. Bless the Lord all my soul and all that is within me, bless Your Holy Name! Thank You Father. I love you so much!

~ Circling The Prayer Wagons! ~

Several friends have amazing faith in the midst of serious illnesses and daily trials. E-mails, texts, phone calls, or messages pass between us as we partner in prayer for strength, healing, and every need.

We've referred to our prayer requests as circling the prayer wagon. Regardless of any attack, we have seen God's hand work mighty wonders.

Jesus said, that where two or three are gathered together that He is there with them (Mathew 18:20).

There is power in prayer, power in praying for one another, and power when we pray together. So when you are under attack, call for reinforcements and circle those prayer wagons!

Heavenly Father I'm calling on You and calling my friends to circle the wagons. Thank You that when the enemy attacks we can run into Your strong arms and always be safe.

~ Team Hope ~

Idaho Public Television aired a program on Adventure Racing. The television crew followed a four person team through sixty-three miles of biking, twenty-two miles on foot, nineteen miles of kayaking across a lake (complete with a storm and lightning), and a frigid swim across Button Hook Bay. Not only do the competitors have to complete this grueling course, but also find a series of mandatory checkpoints and optional controls. Whew!

Team members encourage one another, talking, keeping tabs on each person's progress – both mentally and physically. The race can't be completed alone, and each member is needed.

Life's challenges often stack up like an Adventure Race, and the trials seem daunting. I have friends who recently lost loved ones, some who struggle daily with pain and illness, and others who need help or a listening ear. The needs stretch far and wide.

We weren't meant to travel these roads alone. No matter who you are, you have a purpose. We need you on the team to love and be loved. Whether in person, through letters, e-mails, phone calls, messages, or in prayer – you are needed.

There is life to live and a race to run. Encourage one another, and keep the dialogue open both horizontally and vertically. Stay prayerfully alert. Have eyes, hands, feet, and ears ready at all times to give and receive Christ's love.

My friend, you are on the team. The race may seem daunting at times, but you are never alone, never without hope, always loved, and forever safe on God's Team.

Heavenly Father thank You that in the race of life I'm on Your heavenly winning team!

~ Forget But Remember ~

Are we forgetting the things we should remember, and remembering the things we should forget?

Remember means to call up to mind, bring to remembrance, to make alive again, to attend to, to preserve the memory of; to preserve from being forgotten, to mention, to put in mind; to remind; as, to remember one of his duty, to think of and consider; to meditate.

Forget means to lose the remembrance of, or to let go from the memory.

I don't want to remember (make alive again, preserve the memory of, esteem, or hold with praise, admiration or celebrate) the negative things in my past. I want to forget (let go from the memory) and move toward the future.

I want to remember to praise God for He forgives and forgets my sin. I don't want to forget the cost Jesus paid for my salvation. I want to always remember that God's mercies are new every morning.

I want to follow God fully. God who remembers His covenant, remembers His people. He remembers.

Remember. Remember that God never forgets about you. Remember He rescued you, saved you, and redeemed you. Remember His promise, His power, His might, His love, His faithfulness. Remember!

Don't remember the former things; nor consider the things of old. God is doing a new thing! Now it springs forth. He will make a way in the wilderness and rivers in the desert. Forgetting what is behind and straining toward what is ahead, press on toward the goal to win the prize for which God has called me heavenward in Christ Jesus. (Isaiah 43:18-19, Philippians 3:13-14)

~ *Station The Garrison!* ~

If we worry, fret, and focus on the things of this world, we lose our perspective. We can also lose hope. We start to measure what we have, and who we are, by the world's standards. Thus clouding and muddling our brains and hearts by an earthly perspective.

However when we garrison our hearts and minds by God's truth, we live in the freedom to walk in His wisdom and peace.

So friends, post the guards and mount the garrison!

Take heed, and guard your life diligently. Keep and guard your heart with all vigilance, for out of it flow the springs of life. Let your eyes look right on with fixed purpose, and let your gaze be straight before you. Be attentive to godly wisdom learned by actual and costly experience. Incline your ear to My understanding that you may exercise proper discrimination and discretion and your lips may guard and keep knowledge and the wise answer to temptation.

Don't fret or have any anxiety about anything, but in every circumstance and in everything, by prayer and petition, with thanksgiving, continue to make your wants known to God. And God's peace shall be yours, so fearing nothing from God and being content with its earthly lot of whatever sort that is, that peace which transcends all understanding shall garrison and mount guard over your hearts and minds in Christ Jesus. (Deuteronomy 4:9, Proverbs 4:23, Proverbs 4:25, Proverbs 5:1-2, Philippians 4:6-7)

~ *Wrinkles And Pimples* ~

The mirror doesn't always make me happy. Wrinkles are now obvious, and to add insult to injury I still get pimples. Goodness, I think I'm trapped between puberty and menopause.

Spiritually I have the same problem. I think I'm getting older and wiser, but continue to make decisions which could be deemed childish. Maybe that's just part of the growth process. The closer I move toward God, the more I see my flaws, and the more I realize His constant guidance and presence are needed.

As long as I remain on this earth, I'll keep aging and unfortunately wrinkling, but hopefully growing closer to God.

I do wish that as we aged we would just get cuter and smarter. Perhaps with eternal reality that is true. Our earthly journey is only part of the picture. We age on earth, to be young and our best in Heaven. Oh my, I like that thought!

Heavenly Father, thank You that no matter how old our age on earth, You see us as Your precious children. Help us to mature in our growth with You by studying Your word and spending time with You. I'm so thankful that when our time here on earth is done, You will welcome us home with a new non-pimply, non-wrinkling body!

~ Erased ~

With the blessings of producing and hosting Living Joyfully Free radio, I have acquired new skills. I have the wonderful option of editing out any mistakes. With my handy-dandy audio program, I highlight the offending area, hit delete, and poof! My flubs are gone never to be found again. My file is then saved nice and clean. Ah the power!

While pondering the past, God brought up some important truths. When we ask God forgiveness for our sins and truly repent, those sins are erased. They are gone.

God promises He has swept away our offenses like a cloud, our sins like the morning mist. He has removed our sins as far as the east is from the west.

Through Jesus we have forgiveness of sins through the riches of God's grace. He promises to be and never again remember our sins

If you have asked forgiveness, God not only forgives, He forgets.

God who can't lie, has promised He has forgiven AND forgotten (erased) any past sins which we have brought to Him.

God's mercies are new every morning. You are free to walk free. You don't have to drag around the past. You are free and safe and sound in God's love.

"For God so greatly loved and dearly prized the world that He [even] gave up His only begotten (unique) Son, so that whoever believes in (trusts in, clings to, relies on) Him shall not perish (come to destruction, be lost) but have eternal (everlasting) life.

"For God did not send the Son into the world in order to judge (to reject, to condemn, to pass sentence on) the world, but that the world might find salvation and be made safe and sound through Him." ~ John 3:16-17 (AMP)

~ Isaiah 44:22, Psalm 103:11-12, Acts 13:38, Ephesians 1:7, Hebrews 8:12

·

~ Eye Have A Problem ~

Interesting how our bodies work, isn't it? The smallest thing like a paper cut can cause pain. For some reason a sore formed on my eye like a blister—clear and raised. The doctor said the condition is chronic. If treatment is ignored, the wound grows, leaves scar tissue, and eventually causes blindness.

At this point, the scarring isn't obvious, only a discoloration and lightening on the damaged section of the cornea. Pain and tenderness are the only symptoms. However that does get my attention, and helps remind me to take care of the problem.

Sin is similar to a blister. Sometimes they aren't very obvious and are easy to ignore. Until the pain starts.

Sin leaves scarring — tiny or huge damages to our souls and/or bodies. Whether the wounds are caused by the sins of others or self-inflicted, the scarring remains. Pain is a reminder to change and seek treatment. Thankfully, we have a God who heals all wounds.

God is the God who can overcome any and all temptation to sin. God stands with open arms for those truly seeking grace. And God has the perfect ointment, and the perfect salve for any and all damage. Got sin? God is the answer.

Heavenly Father thank You for Your grace that removes the blisters of sin.

~ Grumbles ~

It is so easy to get a bad attitude and start complaining and grumbling about life, politics, the economy, people, climate, health issues, the weather, the traffic, anything and everything.

But when we grumble, we lose.

We lose pieces of ourselves and opportunities to notice the good in life. We lose eyes to see God working.

Grumbles kill, steal, and destroy. They kill hope. Steal joy. Destroy attitudes.

Grumbling leads to fruitless wandering blocking God's blessings.

Grumbles see only the negatives.

Grumbling makes us, and everyone around us, miserable.

God's way is the best way. When we keep our focus on God, choosing to walk in faith, trusting and knowing He is in control and His loving care transcends any earthly situation, the grumbles dissipate in Christ's peace.

"Do all things without grumbling or disputing. In everything give thanks; for this is God's will for you in Christ Jesus. Be anxious for nothing, but in everything by prayer and supplication with thanksgiving let your requests be made known to God. And the peace of God, which surpasses all comprehension, will guard your hearts and your minds in Christ Jesus." ~ Philippians 2:14, 1 Thessalonians 5:18, Philippians 4:6-7 (NASB)

~ Self Wrestling ~

I woke before 4:00 in the morning, and the worries of the day attacked. So much to do, so little time, how would I get everything done?

I need help, God. Please show me what to do. Help me get everything done. Help my family, help my friends, help me. Me ... me ... me ... me....

By the time the alarm went off, me, myself, and I were exhausted. Whew! Self wrestling isn't a pretty sport. Someone always loses, and that someone is me.

Prayer is a wonderful thing, especially when remembering that God is in control—that requests are heard, and He is sufficient for all needs. I pulled up my little proverbial bootstraps, remembering that I can do everything through Him who gives me strength.

Problem was, I was emphasizing the "I" in the verse. I wasn't emphasizing The One who gives me the strength. It's not by my power or anything I can do, everything can be accomplished by God's strength. God is able to give us all the grace we need, so that we have all we need for every need.

Boy is that easier! I can always rely on God and I don't have to rely on me.

Thank You, Father that You are the source of strength. You provide the grace, You provide all we need, and You are at work in us for Your good purpose. Thank You Father, thank You!

~ Philippians 4:13, 2 Corinthians 9:8

~ Flailing ~

Have you ever been in a body of water completely panicked, with arms flailing, thinking you're drowning, when in reality all you had to do was lower your feet and stand?

I've been there, done that. Rather embarrassing, but very comforting when those toes touch sand or terra firma.

Which got me to wondering, how many times as Christians do we flounder, flap, and flail in the midst of our circumstances?

How often do we forget Jesus gives eternal life and no one can snatch us out of His hand? And no one can snatch us out of the Father's hand. Stop, rest, think about, and relish that wonderful truth.

No matter what difficulties we face, we really are always safe in God's hands and firmly planted in His love. When we take the time to be still, and remember God is in control, our flailing stops.

Be still in Hebrew means to sink down, let drop, be quiet, or relax. How awesome we can lean back, confident in the palm of God's Hands. We are always held secure in the loving hands of Jesus.

"I give eternal life to them, and they will never perish; and no one will snatch them out of My hand. My Father, who has given them to Me, is greater than all; and no one is able to snatch them out of the Father's hand." ~ John 10:28-29 (NASB)

~ Flesh Coddler ~

When we focus only on our needs, all we see are our needs, and we miss other's needs. When we focus only on ourselves, we miss seeing blessings, and we miss being a blessing. When we focus only on our abilities, we miss the ability to see beyond our abilities to see God's abilities. When we focus only on our flesh, coddling the flesh, wanting the flesh to save, we miss The Savior.

When we focus on our self, we are locked in self-pity, self-entitlement, and self-reliance, and we miss the blessings of dying to self to fully live in Christ. When we focus on God, exalt God, the more we see His provision, His blessings, His abilities, His saving grace, might, and abundant life.

"Those who think they can do it on their own end up obsessed with measuring their own moral muscle but never get around to exercising it in real life.

"Those who trust God's action in them find that God's Spirit is in them—living and breathing God! Obsession with self in these matters is a dead end; attention to God leads us out into the open, into a spacious, free life.

"Focusing on the self is the opposite of focusing on God. Anyone completely absorbed in self ignores God, ends up thinking more about self than God. That person ignores who God is and what he is doing. And God isn't pleased at being ignored. So we fix our eyes not on what is seen, but on what is unseen. For what is seen is temporary, but what is unseen is eternal. Therefore, fix your thoughts on Jesus. Fix our eyes on Jesus, the author and perfecter of our faith." ~ Romans 8:5 MSG, 2 Corinthians 4:18, Hebrews 3:1, 12:2 (NIV)

~ Pity Party ~

I'll admit I have moments when I struggle with past issues. Not just what I've been through, but what I've done. The past rears its ugly head in the daylight, others creep into dreams in the night, but both leave me struggling to regain a firm footing.

If I'm not careful, the dreaded pity party comes to call, complete with an abundance of whine and chocolate. Maybe I'll even put on a sad song so the tears flow freely. "Poor me" I say in my best whiney voice, please pass the chocolate.

As tempting as it may be to wallow in the muck of the past, there are choices. Oswald Chambers advised to "take ourselves by the scruff of the neck and shake ourselves" out of our moods. Goodness knows there are days I need a good shaking.

We are not left defenseless against these assaults, there are weapons—God and His word. God blesses us with new mercies and opportunities. What's done is done, but what is to come through our Savior, is new, vibrant, and exciting. Jesus—the Way, the Truth, and the Life, Prince of Peace, Lord of Lords—rescues us from our sins, the pain of yesterday, and gives hope for tomorrow.

Pity party over, I'm dusting off the past and moving forward.

Heavenly Father help me to stop looking back at the past and keep my focus on the vibrant, exciting future with You!

~ Get Out Of The Self Processor ~

Have you ever noticed how much time is spent on self-processing?

We process our past. We process what we said. We process what someone else said. We process what is happening in our lives and the world around us. We process fear and worry. We process ourselves and everyone we meet. We process until our brains are scrambled by processing.

Ack!

Fortunately with the help of God's word we can climb out of the self-processor.

Cast your burden on the Lord, and He will sustain you. He won't ever permit the righteous to be moved. For God didn't give us a spirit of fear but has given us a spirit of power and of love and of calm and well-balanced mind and discipline and self-control. So let's think about the things that are good and worthy of praise. Think about the things that are true and honorable and right and pure and beautiful and respected. And God who gives peace will be with you (Psalm 55:22, 2 Timothy 1:7, Philippians 4:8-9).

Heavenly Father, help me to stop the self-processing. Help me to stay in Your word. I'm casting my burdens on You remembering You keep my mind at peace when I keep my focus on You. Help me to stop thinking about me and think about You and the things that are true, honorable, right, pure, beautiful, and respected.

~ Out Of The Groove ~

What if during an MRI, doctors could not only see the tissues of the brain, but also see inside each groove? And what if each groove highlighted the thoughts contained within?

Habits and thoughts literally grind ruts in the brain similar to the ridges in vinyl records. The more something is repeated, the deeper the channel. Bad thoughts and habits create valleys, the walls of which are steep and difficult to climb. Good thoughts and memories bring pleasant furrows, providing a place of nurturing and growth.

Bad ruts and memories sometimes take us down dark pathways. Fortunately the brain is malleable, and we can reroute those thought patterns replacing them with God's truth.

I love the Message version of 2 Corinthians 10:5, "We use our powerful God-tools for smashing warped philosophies, tearing down barriers erected against the truth of God, fitting every loose thought and emotion and impulse into the structure of life shaped by Christ."

And Paul reminds us to think on the things that are true, noble, right, pure, lovely, admirable, anything excellent or praiseworthy. Regardless of how I feel, I want my grooves to light up with God's love.

Even if the way is long, hard, and dark, we can form living, vibrant, healthy channels with God's wonderful truth.

We may have groovy brains, travel rut-filled roads, but we have a God who promises to lead us on a straight path—the highway straight to His eternal love.

Heavenly Father help me to get out of the negative ruts by keeping my thoughts positively highlighted with Your loving truth.

~ Is God BIG Enough? ~

I'm saddened by how many Christians seem to be living defeated lives. The past seems too big to overcome, the present seems overwhelming, and the future looms like a tidal wave.

Is God big enough to handle what you face?

The God who created creation. The God who breathes life. The God who fights for you. The God who rescues. The God who can part seas, wide enough for two million people to cross, deep enough to drown an entire Egyptian army.

The God who provides counsel and instruction. The God who is our refuge.

The God whose love is unfailing, peaceful, and compassionate. The God who saves. The God who is all-powerful, all-knowing, just, righteous, loving, true, pure, and holy.

The God who finds nothing too hard or difficult. The God who raises the dead.

The God who loves us so much He offers new life through His Son, Jesus Christ. The God who finds nothing impossible. The God who is above all things.

The God who gives wisdom and knowledge. The God who holds you in the palm of His hand. The God who will never leave or forsake you. The God who is the beginning and the end.

The God who is the way, the truth, and the life. The God who is present in the past, present, and future.

Now…

Is. your. God. **BIG**. enough. to handle whatever you face?

Heavenly Father I know You are big enough for anything and everything! Lord I believe, help my unbelief.

~ Genesis 1, Genesis 2:7, Exodus 14:14-31, Deuteronomy 31:6, Psalm 16:7, Psalm 20:6, Psalm 91:9, Psalm 97:9, Proverbs 2:6, Isaiah 49:16, Isaiah 54:10, Jeremiah 29:11, Jeremiah 32:27, Luke 1:37, John 3:16, John 11:1-44, John 14:6, Revelation 1:8, Revelation 16:7, Revelation 22:13

~ All In ~

I messed up. I sent a friend a possible devotion to use on her site, and then realized I can do better. More can be done. I can open my heart fully and let the love of The Father pour through my feeble soul.

God has called me to write, blog, and share the testimonies of other to a hurting and lost world. And at times I step tentative, pull back, or go with what is easy, instead of diving in deep.

I asked my Father for forgiveness. I wrote and asked my friend for her forgiveness. And I ask the same of you, please forgive me.

I want to be ALL IN.

All in to share my Father's love. All in to do my best through God's power, grace, mercy, and strength. I want to offer my best to Him. I don't want to lose sight of God and my calling. And the only way I can keep my focus on Him is spending time with Him and His word.

All in means living in the now – not in the past or the future. Living in the moment with our God who is the great I AM. He is here, now. Don't lose your moment.

Be All In with The One who is ALL.

"Lean on, trust in, and be confident in the Lord with all your heart and mind and do not rely on your own insight or understanding. In all your ways know, recognize, and acknowledge Him, and He will direct and make straight and plain your paths." ~ Proverbs 3:5-6 (AMP)

~ IN-Joy ~

I've been pondering the wonderful God-given gift of joy. There are so many mentions of joy throughout God's word. I love that God's joy isn't a happy feeling based on circumstances.

We are told that in God's presence is fullness of joy. Our God is a joyous refuge from trouble. And when we receive Christ who is Immanuel—God with us—we not only receive Christ, but the fullness of God's joy.

We have joy that God loves us. Joy that Jesus Christ was born for us. Wonderful joy, that in Jesus Christ we are offered salvation. Amazing joy, that Jesus lives in all those who receive and believe in Him.

Joy that we are given the Holy Spirit to reside in us and the Holy Spirit blesses us with the fruit of the Spirit which includes joy. In Christ we have eternal hope. In Christ we receive deliverance. In Christ we are restored. In Christ we are renewed. In Christ we live IN JOY!

Consider all the ways you have been blessed with opportunities to enjoy (in joy) life. And more importantly consider the joy of knowing your eternal future is secure. Substitute your name in the verses below and make each joyful promise your own.

Let all who take refuge and put their trust in You rejoice; let them ever sing and shout for joy, because You make a covering over them and defend them. Let those who love Your name be joyful in You. You will show me the path of life; in Your presence is fullness of joy, at Your right hand are pleasures forevermore. You have told us these things so that we will be filled with Your joy. Yes, our joy will overflow! (Psalm 5:11, Psalm 16:11, John 15:11)

~ Road-Map To Freedom ~

The Bible isn't a book of rules and regulations; it is a road-map to freedom.

His Word shows us the way ... Give me Your lantern and compass, give me a map, so I can find my way to the sacred mountain, to the place of Your presence. The signposts of God are clear and point out the right road. The life-maps of God are right, showing the way to joy. The directions of God are plain and easy on the eyes.

How can a young person live a clean life? By carefully reading the map of your Word. I'm single-minded in pursuit of you; don't let me miss the road signs you've posted.

Dear friend, take my advice; it will add years to your life. I'm writing out clear directions to Wisdom Way, I'm drawing a map to Righteous Road. Jesus is the way, the truth, and the life; no one comes to the Father but through Him. And in Him you will know the truth, and the truth will make you free. And if the Son makes you free, you are free indeed.

Heavenly Father thank You for Your Word and truth which is our road-map to freedom.

~ Psalm 43:3-4 MSG, Psalm 19:7-8, Psalm 119:9-16,Proverbs 4:10-15 MSG, John 14:6, 8:32, 8:36 NASB.

~ Hearing You ~

You whisper in my heart, "*Come away my beloved.*"

My heart moans with longing, and I tear myself from the shackles and constraints placed on myself and my busyness. I come into Your presence where You wait with open arms. Your Holy Spirit envelopes, and breathes, and rains on my thirsty soul.

And I try so hard, so very hard, to block the noises of the day and the things that keep me from Your side. The things that are blessings yet can become such chains to chain me on the earth and keep me from flying to Your presence.

O Heavenly Father, muffle the sounds from within and without. Shield my soul from what drives me away from You. Nothing on earth, no one on earth, no possession, title, or accomplishment, can replace You. Whom have I in heaven and on earth besides You?

I love You, Father. Forever. Take my mind, body, heart, soul, and strength. I give my all to You. Your loving child.

~ Bogus ~

My sweet husband and I drove to Bogus Basin Ski Resort. During the off-season months the area is open to hikers and bikers. We parked in one of the areas at the 6000 foot level, and using the ski and snowshoe trails hiked to the top -- 7582 feet! Woo hoo!

I've decided that life as a Christ follower is a narrow, curvy path. We never know what's around the next bend, but we know Who is leading the way.

Some days are fun like playing "peek-a-boo" and the turn in the road is delightful. Other days seem like fifty foot drops into gravel pits, but God is always there to mend the wounds and heal the scars. With God, life is never boring and always an adventure.

My prayer is, show me Your ways Lord, show me Your paths (Psalm 25:4).

Regardless how rocky the road gets, God is always there. I love that He promises, to keep us safe in His dwelling, He will hide us in the shelter of His tabernacle and set us high upon a rock (Psalm 27:5).

And the most awesome thing about life as a Christian is that God will always lead us safely home. And that my friend, is no bogus message. :)

Heavenly Father thank You for the journey with You. Thank You that even when the way is fun, rough, or scary, You never lead us on a bogus journey.

~ Whacked Out ~

Three feet into edging and weed-whacking our yard, our "self-feeding" weed-eater stopped feeding. I turned over the contraption, took off the cap, manually pulled the string, reassembled, turned it over, and succeeded in sprucing up another two feet. Again, the equipment failed to provide additional string.

Being of the stubborn variety and not wanting to spend money on another weed-eater, my fifteen minute task turned into a two-hour ordeal. During this weed-whack/edge scenario, I wondered if perhaps God wasn't trying to teach me something other than patience.

I knew the answer before I asked. During the last month, my quiet time had not been the length I've wanted or needed. I sit at God's feet, soak for about ten minutes, hit the ground running and collapse about two feet later. Projects pull at me from various directions and progress is minimal, slow, and frustrating.

My remaining time in the yard, I spent asking God for direction and guidance. What do I need to do with my writing? Which projects are most important? Finally finished, I took the tools in the garage.

Out of the corner of my eye I noticed someone walk by on the sidewalk. A moment later, our doorbell rang. I stepped out and found a little boy probably no older than six. Wearing jeans and a flannel shirt, he stood in front of me holding a basket with small loaves of poppy seed bread. He was too cute to resist. Transaction complete, I leaned down to thank him. His eyes met mine and my heart melted.

When he left, I prayed for him and his family—prayed they would know Jesus. And in the quiet of my soul knew the answer to my questions. The projects I had been given aren't distractions, they are methods to share

God's good news. Grateful, relieved, and exhausted, I sat on the bumper of our car and cried.

Dear Heavenly Father, thank You for Your patience and gentle methods of teaching. Help me to always spend time refueling with You to drink deep of Your truth. And then when I am properly prepared, help me to keep sharing the good news of Your grace, mercy, and love. Please watch over my little friend. Keep him safe and speak to his heart so one day I'll see him again when we are in Heaven enveloped forever in Your love and joy. I love You, Father.

~ Road Tripping ~

When we were in the process of car shopping for our son, we were having a difficult time finding a suitable vehicle. At the time he was six foot five inches tall in his stocking feet. (He is now six foot eight). Even though he's thin, he couldn't even squeeze in the seat of some of the smaller cars. So, we considered bequeathing my sweet hubby's Jeep to sweet son and maybe us getting something else.

The pocketbook advised something cheap, so I tried out a little car that was rather fun to drive. I'll admit feeling like a teenager, which led to those youthful thoughts that I really needed a pin stripe and sporty wheels, maybe even a stereo with big speakers in back so I could blast out my praise music as I rocked down the road.

The adult in me wanted safe, affordable, easy on the insurance rates, and one that would last a LONG time without need for repairs. Ugh. I hate spending money. I really want God to place a flashing neon sign over the vehicle he wanted us to buy saying "buy this one."

Of course, I would love that kind of sign on everything I do. Wouldn't it be cool to wake with a day-timer already filled out by God? I would zoom around checking off things, pleasing God, and I'd be happy and fulfilled.

True, except for that nasty side of me that would be a touch rebellious. I'd probably check the day-timer, decide perhaps other things could fit into my schedule, and wind up driving off-road looking for flowers, rivers, and hills. Then I'd race back feeling horribly guilty.

Bummer. Even without my daily God schedule, I can give myself a big guilt trip.

So, what did I do? Whined. Whimpered. Stared at the computer screen. Stared outside. Stared at my dog. Stared at my Bible....

Eureka! Answers!

He has showed you, what is good. What does the LORD require of you? To act justly and to love mercy and to walk humbly with your God. Whether you turn to the right or to the left, you'll hear a voice behind you, saying, this is the way; walk in it. I guide you in the way of wisdom and lead you along straight paths (Micah 6:8, Isaiah 30:21, Proverbs 4:11).

Thank You Father, for Your word. Thank You for Your promises and guidance. Please forgive me when I get stuck in ruts or drive off with my own agenda. Help me to listen for Your voice, follow Your teachings, remember that You are always in control, and enjoy this wild road trip called life.

~ Battle Plan ~

Waking with a start, mind reeling, I ran for my Bible. In my nightmare, people/monsters grabbed me, trying to drag me away to their monstrous world. My method of escape was to use the sword of the spirit – scripture.

Even during the dream I knew I was in trouble. How quickly could I quote verses, how many could I remember in rapid fire, were they appropriate for my situation and would they make the enemy turn and run?

If your only weapon was God's Word, would you be prepared to battle?

Below is a listing of scripture, truth with which to stand firm and escape the grasp of the enemy. Search in your own Bible to find your Battle plan.

"The Lord is my strength and song, and He has become my salvation; this is my God, and I will praise Him; my father's God, and I will extol Him. The Lord is a warrior; the Lord is His name." ~ Exodus 15:2-3 (NASB)

"The LORD himself will fight for you. Just stay calm." ~ Exodus 14:14 (NLT)

"The eternal God is your refuge, and his everlasting arms are under you. He drives out the enemy before you; he cries out, 'Destroy them!'" ~ Deuteronomy 33:27 (NLT)

"The God of my strength, in whom I will trust; my shield and the horn of my salvation, my stronghold and my refuge; my Savior, You save me from violence." ~ 2 Samuel 22:3 (NKJV)

"As for God, His way is blameless; the word of the Lord is tested; He is a shield to all who take refuge in Him." ~ 2 Samuel 22:31 (NASB)

Lord, you bless those who do what is right; you protect them like a soldier's shield." ~ Psalm 5:12 (NCV)

"The Lord is my rock, my fortress, and my savior; my God is my rock, in whom I find protection. He is my shield, the power that saves me, and my place of safety." ~ Psalm 18:2 (NLT)

"The Lord is my light and my salvation—so why should I be afraid? The Lord is my fortress, protecting me from danger, so why should I tremble?" ~ Psalm 27:1 (NLT)

"We are completely victorious through God who showed his love for us. Yes, I am sure that neither death, nor life, nor angels, nor ruling spirits, nothing now, nothing in the future, no powers, nothing above us, nothing below us, nor anything else in the whole world will ever be able to separate us from the love of God that is in Christ Jesus our Lord." ~ Romans 8:37-39 (NCV)

"So what should we say about this? If God is for us, no one can defeat us." ~ Romans 8:31 (NCV)

Heavenly Father thank You for Your word that gives us power over the enemy, power over any circumstance, and power to live in Your freedom.

~ God's Love Letters To You — You Are Loved! ~

I created your inmost being and knit you together in your mother's womb. I take delight in you. I quiet you with My love. I rejoice over you with singing. I am gracious, righteous and full of compassion. I have loved you with an everlasting love, and I have drawn you with loving-kindness. I will make known to you the path of life. In My presence is fullness of joy, in My right hand there are pleasures forever. Though the mountains are shaken and the hills removed, My unfailing love for you will not be shaken nor will My covenant of peace be removed.

I know the plans I have for you, plans to prosper you and not to harm you, plans to give you hope and a future. When you call to Me and come and pray to Me, I will listen to you. You will seek Me and find Me when you seek Me with all your heart. And I will be found by you. See, I have engraved you on the palms of my hands.

In My unfailing love I will lead you. In My strength I will guide you to My holy dwelling. I loved you so much that I gave My one and only Son, so that when you believed in Him you would have eternal life. And My Son came so that you would have life, and have it abundantly.

My love is patient, kind, does not envy, does not boast, is not proud, rude, or self-seeking, is not easily angered, and keeps no record of wrongs. My love does not delight in evil but rejoices with the truth. It always protects, always trusts, always hopes, always perseveres. My love never fails. I am love, and I love you. ~ Your Heavenly Father.

~ Psalm 139:13, Zephaniah 3:17, Psalm 149:4, Psalm 116:5, Jeremiah 31:3, Psalm 16:11, Isaiah 54:10, Jeremiah 29:11-14, Isaiah 49:16, Exodus 15:13, John 3:16, John 10:10, Deuteronomy 7:13

~ The Starting Pistol ~

Picture a track meet at the Olympics. The athletes are in position in the starting blocks. The starting pistol fires. What if no one moved, no one ran?

I wonder if we as Christians have become adept at pew sitting, instead of running the race. It's so easy to sit in our holy huddles for church, Bible study, and small groups. We are careful who we socialize with in person and in our social circles.

However, Jesus said go, tell, and make disciples. Be salt and light and spread the good news.

If we only sit and stew, or bring stew to our Christian potluck dinners, we won't help feed those starving for God's truth.

The starting pistol has fired. Let's get fired up about taking Christ's message to the world!

"Therefore go and make disciples of all nations, baptizing them in the name of the Father and of the Son and of the Holy Spirit, and teaching them to obey everything I have commanded you. And surely I am with you always, to the very end of the age. Let us lay aside every encumbrance and the sin which so easily entangles us, and let us run with endurance the race that is set before us, fixing our eyes on Jesus, the author and perfecter of faith." ~ Matthew 28:19-20 (NIV), Hebrews 12:1-2 (NASB)

~ *Unanswered Or Unbound?* ~

Most of us have heard or experienced, amazing stories of God's answered prayers. The checks arriving in the mail at just the right time, the groceries left on the doorstep when the pantry was bare, the lights that shine in the darkest hours.

But what of prayers that seem to go unanswered? The struggles that don't stop. The onslaught that keeps onslaughting, the times when heaven seems silent.

The times we question, and agonize, and wonder, where is God and why He doesn't answer?

Are prayers more than we realize?

God is omnipotent, omnipresent, and not limited by space and time. He is, and was, and is to come. He is the great I AM.

Prayers are timeless in God's hands. Unbound by earth's laws they float like incense to Heaven's door.

Prayers ripple throughout eternity. Every drop unwasted, gathering, growing, bursting through barriers, setting captives free, delivering nourishment to the weary, protection, provision, and a never-ending breath of God's grace, mercy, and love.

Keep praying. Each prayer, every whispered plea, matters for now and eternity. Keep praying.

Heavenly Father thank You that no prayer goes unanswered, help me to continue praying knowing Your divine will unbounds and unleashes Your perfect purpose in my life and in the lives of others.

~ 168 Hours ~

"Rejoice always; pray without ceasing; in everything give thanks; for this is God's will for you in Christ Jesus."
~ 1 Thessalonians 5:16-18 (NASB)

There are 168 hours in each week. How much time do you spend watching television, playing video games, reading the news, wasting time? How much time do you spend with God? How much time do you spend with The Good News?

Church attendance... 0-3 hours?
Bible study... 0-3 hours?
Prayer at meals, bedtime, quiet time... 0-3 hours?

How much time are you spending on what is eternal? How much time do you want to spend with God? How much time can we spend? How much time <u>will</u> we spend with God?

How much time do we want God to spend with us?

Don't miss the time to spend time on the best time with The One who makes all time.

Heavenly Father, show us how to use our time better to be in Your Word, in Your presence, in prayer to have a vital, growing relationship with You. O Father, I want You in every moment, and all the times of my life!

~ What Do You Want To Talk About? ~

What if someone came to your door every day at 7:00 in the morning and 10:00 at night? What if every time they came to visit, they talked nonstop telling you everything they wanted and needed? They never wanted to hear what you had to say, and anytime you tried to respond, they interrupted.

Would you consider that person a true friend?

Don't we do the same thing with God? We come with our lists of needs and wants, but how often do we come quietly and ask, "God, what would you like to talk about today?"

God is waiting and wants to talk with you. Lay your list of wants and needs aside, and take time; make time, to listen to God.

When we come to God in prayer, do we bring our list? Or will we bring ourselves?

My sheep listen to My voice; I know them, and they follow Me. Whoever is of God listens to God. Those who belong to God hear the words of God. (John 10:27, John 8:47)

~ Hardwired For Praise ~

Do we greet our family, friends, and pets with more enthusiasm than we greet God? Do we think more about ourselves and our situations than we think of God?

Is the focus on what others do and say, more than what God says in His word and the amazing ways He works in His people?

Down in our DNA, the marrow of our bones, we are hardwired for praise and thanksgiving. Every breath we breathe is a gift, and every breath can be filled with praise.

For in a thankful heart we are blessed with God's joy and presence, which blesses us with joy and His presence, which blesses God, which blesses us, which blesses Him, which blesses us, which blesses Him, which blesses us …

In God's economy, you can never out-give God. The more we seek Him, we find Him. The more we hunger and thirst for righteousness, we will be filled. The closer we draw to Him, the closer He draws to us. The more praise and thanksgiving we give Him, the more our spirits are uplifted and renewed.

If you are feeling powerless and weak, plug into your Creator through praise. If you are feeling thankful, plug into your Creator through praise. Regardless of how you are feeling, plug into your Creator through praise.

"Oh, what joy for those whose disobedience is forgiven, whose sin is put out of sight! Yes, what joy for those whose record the LORD has cleared of guilt!

So rejoice in the LORD and be glad, all you who obey Him! Shout for joy, all you whose hearts are pure! May all who search for You be filled with joy and gladness in You.

May those who love Your salvation repeatedly shout, 'The LORD is great!' For in Your presence is fullness of joy, at Your right hand there are pleasures forevermore."

~ Psalm 32:1-2 (NLT), Psalm 32:11 (NLT), Psalm 40:16 (NLT), Psalm 16:11 (AMP)

~ Compelled By Love ~

I've blogged for years. For a certain time period I was compelled to write daily. Then the compulsion was removed. God granted freedom. So I stepped back.

But the flame didn't dim. And as Jeremiah wrote, "there is in my heart as it were a burning fire shut up in my bones, and I am weary with holding it in, and *I cannot.*"

The fire stayed in my heart. If I don't tell others about God's love *I am miserable.* I am driven by a compulsion of love that burns to share God's Good News. The good news of a tender, loving, compassionate God. A God who offers forgiveness and restoration through His Son, Jesus Christ. A Savior who saves.

His grace and mercy are available to all who will answer His loving knock on the door of their hearts.

Don't waste a moment. Time is short. The time is now. Open your heart to His call. Fan into flame the gift of God's passion in your heart. Spend time with God and The Living Word. And you too will say, "Did not our hearts burn within us while he talked to us on the road, while he opened to us the Scriptures?"

For in God's presence we find our individual, unique, loving compulsion.

How is God's love compelling you?

~ Jeremiah 20:9, 2 Timothy 1:6, Luke 24:32

~ *Nothing and No One* ~

Reason sees only with earthly eyes clouded with earthly vision. Emotions flail with the whispering winds of lies from the enemy, society, media, and those who surround us and live in the flesh.

There is nothing that lasts. There is no peace, no joy, no stability, no hope, and no truth apart from God. There is nothing that can provide meaning and no one who can provide everlasting life apart from Jesus Christ. Nothing matches our matchless Savior, and no one is like our God!

"There is no one like the God of Israel. He rides across the heavens to help you, across the skies in majestic splendor. And I am convinced that nothing can ever separate us from God's love. Neither death nor life, neither angels nor demons, neither our fears for today nor our worries about tomorrow—not even the powers of hell can separate us from God's love." ~ Deuteronomy 33:26 (NLT), Romans 8:38 (NLT)

~ Taking Measurements ~

Have you ever entered a room full of people and immediately checked to make sure you were dressed like everyone else? Or entered a classroom and tried to see the other student's papers to make sure you correctly finished an assignment? Or turned on the television and wished you had "that" car, "that" house, "that" job, or "that"....

Who we are and what we have is constantly under scrutiny. We measure who we are, and what we have, to who others are, and what they have. Whew!

I must admit to chuckling every time I read 2 Corinthians 10:12 in the Amplified version ... "Not that we [have the audacity to] venture to class or [even to] compare ourselves with some who exalt and furnish testimonials for themselves! However, when they measure themselves with themselves and compare themselves with one another, they are without understanding and behave unwisely"

Thankfully God gave us each callings and gifts "for the equipping of the saints for the work of ministry, for the edifying of the body of Christ, till we all come to the unity of the faith and of the knowledge of the Son of God, to a perfect man, to the measure of the stature of the fullness of Christ."(Ephesians 4:12-13 NKJV)

I'm so grateful God's measurements aren't taken by the world's standards, but through the grace of Jesus Christ.

Heavenly Father thank You that when You look at me, You see Your perfect Son who lives in my heart. Thank You that because of the sacrifice and mercy of Jesus, I measure up to stand in Your presence.

~ Excuse Me God, Can We Talk? ~

When our dog was a puppy, he escaped whenever we opened our front door. He thoroughly enjoyed the chase as his family screamed like wild people for him to stop. One getaway occurred when my husband and I were in need of surgeries and our son had asthma. The puppy was the only healthy one in the bunch.

The three of us fanned out, hoping to catch our puppy before he got too far.

I found myself praying, "God, I'm sorry to bother You, but could You help us catch him?"

We knew God would help; we just weren't sure how far we'd have to hobble. After a painful, wheezing chase, our pup was cornered on the front porch of a neighbor's house.

When we returned home, puppy safe in our son's strong arms, I realized my prayer had been tentative. And I wondered, why the hesitation?

Paul, in Philippians 4:6, tell us to pray about everything. Small children request anything and everything. Maybe as adults we rank our petitions. We are worried our "little" things are not important to a Holy God.

God longs to be involved in every area of our lives, just like I want my family and friends to tell me about their days, not just the major happenings.

Oswald Chambers wrote, *"The meaning of prayer is that we get hold of God, not of the answer."*

Talking to God solidifies our relationship with Him. Keeping that line of communication open drives our roots deeper into the firm ground of His abiding presence.

Your Heavenly Father longs to hear from you. God created you—He never finds you or what is happening in your life insignificant. No prayer is too big or too small. God is never busy or distracted. Talk to Him, He's waiting to listen, even if you're out chasing wayward puppies.

"Do not be anxious about anything, but in everything, by prayer and petition, with thanksgiving, present your requests to God." ~ Philippians 4:6 (NIV)

~ Truly Living ~

Life isn't about living for yourself, or pleasing man, or your own pleasures, or even your earthly life. True life is being about Gods business, telling others, making disciples, leaving the world a better place by pointing others to eternal life through Christ.

Jesus Christ died for you. Will you live for Him? He took your place and paid the ultimate price to set you free.

Will you accept His freedom and tell others about the freedom found in Him? Truly live your life by sharing the truth of the eternal life found in Christ. Now that's living!

"My life is worth nothing to me unless I use it for finishing the work assigned me by the Lord Jesus—the work of telling others the Good News about the wonderful grace of God." ~ Acts 20:24 (NLT)

~ Through Prayer ~

I want to be different and changed for the better with each passing day. I don't want to be stagnant and stuck in the mundane of mere existence. I want more of God—to know Him more completely. Oh to be like Enoch who walked with God, or David—a person after God's own heart. Or like Moses who spoke to God face-to-face, and when he stepped from God's presence, his face glowed.

Are these just some mere fantasies? Can those of us who aren't in the Bible, who aren't called by God to do miraculous signs and wonders, live beyond ordinary lives while still living in the ordinary?

Yes!

All around us, right now at this moment, there are people making ripples in eternity. Regardless of age, social standing, race, creed, or color, they work in amazing ways for the Kingdom of God.

Through prayer, they empower evangelists. Through prayer, they guide the surgeon's hand. Through prayer, they hedge protection around their friends and family members. Through prayer, they surround the grieving with comfort and peace. Through prayer, they dive deeper into God's presence. Through prayer, their hearts radiate with God's love. Through prayer, we can do more, be more, and grow more. And through prayer, we can all make a difference.

"Be unceasing in prayer praying perseveringly."~ 1 Thessalonians 5:17 (AMP)

~ Keeping Score ~

What if we only kept score of the good things?

Sports fans of Babe Ruth can tell you his home run record but ignore the enormous times he struck out ~ Home runs = 714 Strike outs = 1330.

Unfortunately we usually make notes of every bad thing that ever happens. The mean thing someone said, the date when our life went down a different path, the day we lost our job, our spouse, our home, the friend we thought would be friends forever.

What if we changed our thinking? What if the only dates we remembered were the good days? What if we kept records of everything good that happened during every day?

We wouldn't have room in our journals or on the hard drives of our computers.

Keeping Score of Today's Good Things

I woke up.
I have food to eat.
I have air to breathe.
I have a place to lay my head tonight.
I have a body that is working.
I can write.
I can read.
I have a family.
I have a permanent family in Christ!
I have a God who loves me!
I have a Savior who saved me!
I can tell others about God's wonderful love!
I have an eternal home in Heaven!
In Christ we always get the happy ending!
I am blessed, so blessed, so very blessed!

Heavenly Father, help me to keep score of the good things. The good that You have done, the good You are doing, the good You will do. Help me to notice, keep score of and remember the good.

~ *I Heard You Call* ~

I heard You call. Just a little whisper. And I rushed about my day thinking of You. But I didn't stop. You called, and I thought I could squeeze You in later by taking care of the things crowding my day.

And I wondered why I felt out of breath, and so alone, and the world seemed so cold.

I'm so sorry.

My house is cleaner, my Facebook, Twitter, and email friends have been answered, but I haven't spent time with You.

And my soul is so sad, because I know I missed Your call. I might have missed something You would have shared in secret. And I know I missed the best part of today. I might have missed the one thing You really wanted me to do – the one thing that would have blessed my socks off.

I'm so sorry.

Oh Heavenly Father, don't let me miss a moment with You.

Your repentant child comes before You begging for Your grace. Thank You that Your mercies are new every morning. Please don't let me miss Your call again.

"Seek the Lord while you can find him. Call on him now while he is near." ~ Isaiah 55:6 (NLT)

~ Saved By A Savior ~

Wendy Saxton is a beautiful young woman with sparkling brown eyes and long brown hair, Cherokee blood tints her skin with a perpetual tan. She exudes God's grace with her warm, friendly smile. We met in Texas through a writer's group, became friends, and with her permission I share a small part of her testimony.

Sexually abused from the time Wendy was seven years old until age fourteen, she was convinced the fastest way to rid her painful childhood was to become an adult. She married her high school algebra teacher as soon as she graduated. The marriage ended eight years later in divorce. .

Michael came into her life when she began job training. He was gentle, kind, with a softness she had never witnessed in a man. But Michael was a heroin addict, and as she put it, she "ran from man-made shelter number one, to man-made shelter number two."

Memories of her abusive past, coupled with her husband's drug use, took them in and out of drug, alcohol, and group therapy programs. Three children later, her marriage torn apart by her husband's drug use, she found work at a chiropractor's office. When the doctor and his wife invited her to church, she accepted, but went with a mindset often taught in 12-step-programs: "Take what you want and leave the rest."

Church was a tough step for Wendy. "Great spirit" and "creator" were the only words she used—the name "God" was way too personal. The pastor's sermons consisted of expounding on one passage of scripture. Taking baby steps like this into God's word gave her a perfect way to learn and grow. Desperately in need of the weekly encouragement, she attended church every Sunday, careful to leave God in her perfectly placed box—

far away from her abusive past. She refused to discuss the experience with God, thinking He didn't prevent the abuse so He couldn't be trusted now.

Her husband desired to see the kids, and reinitiated their relationship. He was more than happy to attend church. Despite their seemingly insurmountable problems, they'd never stopped loving one another.

Outwardly, Wendy's life seemed to be falling into place, but the inner turmoil remained. At this time Wendy was sober, but "drunk with pain." What follows are her own words.

"The coping skills I learned in secular therapy proved to be effective, but they did nothing for the heart of the matter. Why wasn't I healing? I went to church every Sunday, I prayed, and I went to therapy once a week. My 'getting help' only increased the stress in marriage and family. I couldn't quiet the memories. One day it was okay to hug me, the next it wasn't. I'm losing my mind—not healing.

"It didn't take long for me to break my promise to abstain from alcohol. I left therapy one evening, after all the reality I could stand, and drove to the liquor store. I didn't want to heal. I wanted relief. I cried and drank all the way home.

"Finally home, I pulled down the rear-view mirror. Staring back at me was a little girl too broken to be a wife and mother. But sitting in my truck in the driveway totally blitzed on alcohol, something unexpected happened. My guard came down, and I began talking to God about the pain. Tears were finally flowing. I grieved the loss of my innocence and the rejection of my childhood church.

"In the months of attending group therapy, God had remained uninvited to the journey of healing—other than to beg him to get me out of it, or tell him I wasn't ready. The last time I could remember feeling so small when I prayed was as a little girl—a little girl who didn't believe she was loved and protected by God.

"My vow of silence had been broken by an impaired ability to reason. The sun had risen in no-man's-land. Yes, I had been drinking, but God didn't tell me to sober-up and come back later. Instead, He embraced me. The prodigal daughter had begun the journey home—all 110 pounds of me. I was tear streaked and reeked of alcohol, but oh, so ready."

Even as she drank away her sorrow, God in His mercy, compassion, and love reached out to take her in His arms and to give her the hope she never thought she'd find.

Today Wendy has a message for women bound to perpetual heartache and trauma: "He never minimizes the circumstances that break our hearts. We do, when we deny Him access to the pain."

Her memoir, The Jonah Chronicles, is a candid re-telling of her fight for freedom from the effects of abuse, betrayal, and religious rejection.

She is the founder of The Medicine Place, an on-line women's ministry. Using her own experience as a platform, she addresses complex women's issues with respect to anonymity. Addictions gone, memories healed, she found everything she needed in God and the saving of a Savior.

"Then you will call, and the LORD will answer; You will cry, and He will say, 'Here I am,'" ~ Isaiah 58:9 (NASB)

Used by permission by Wendy Saxton. Please listen to Wendy Saxton's testimony on Living Joyfully Free Radio (www.livingjoyfullyfree) and visit her website, www.WendySaxton.com

~ Breathing After God ~

My first breath came from You.
My every breath relies on You.
O for my soul to always breathe after You

If you are willing ('abah*) and obedient, you will eat the best from the land. ~ Isaiah 1:19

Heavenly Father, I long to be completely willing and obedient. I want to breathe after You, consenting to Your will, resting content, willing, yielding, accepting and desiring all that You desire for my life. May every breath I take, every step I make, breathe me further into You.

Are you breathing after God?

*Strong's #14:'abah (pronounced aw-baw') — to breathe after, to be acquiescent:–consent, rest content will, be willing. Brown-Driver-Briggs Hebrew Lexicon: 'âbâh — to be willing, consent, yield to, accept, to desire

~ *Pursuit* ~

There is a hunger, a constant need to be closer to God, a passionate pursuit to be in His presence. A soul-deep longing to be filled with His goodness, mercy, and loving-kindness.

When we hunger and thirst for righteousness, we are filled. His Words breathe life and soul-sustenance. His living water quenches the heart's dry thirst. We draw near to God, He draws near. As we seek, we find. With pursuit of righteousness and unfailing love we find life, righteousness, and honor. Die to self and we are given life eternal.

And in our pursuit, chains are broken, captives released, broken-hearts restored, spiritual eyes opened, and true freedom is found.

Heavenly Father, there is nothing on this earth as wonderful as You. Nothing else fills. No one else can love us with Your love. No one else can satisfy our deepest needs. With all that I am, I pursue and love You.

~ Psalm 63:1, Exodus 33:19, Matthew 5:6, Proverbs 15:9, Proverbs 21:21, Deuteronomy 4:21, Isaiah 55:6, James 4:8, John 6:35, John 6:63, Acts 17:25, John 7:38, Luke 9:23, John 4:14, John 3:15-16, Luke 4:18

~ Downbeat To Upbeat ~

It's so easy to complain about what we don't like. When we complain about the things we don't like about ourselves, our house, our job, our friend, our spouse, our city, our government, etc., then we have trouble focusing on anything else. And when we get down on the negatives, it's like throwing a concrete block on a swimmer. It sinks us and everyone around us. We drown in the downbeats of our day.

We can make the right choices. We can positively choose where we center our attention and the words we speak. We can think on things that are good, true, honorable, just, pure, lovely, commendable, excellent, and worthy of praise. We can make sure our words are good, helpful, and encouraging. And when we chose the positive thoughts and words, we raise a downbeat world (and us) into the upbeat of God's truth.

Heavenly Father, help me to beat the downbeats with the upbeats of You and Your word. Focus my thoughts on You, guard my mouth to only speak what would bring You honor and glory. And as I think of You and speak of You, You lift my downbeats in the upbeat of You!

~ Philippians 4:8, Ephesians 4:29

~ Finding His Presence ~

I wonder sometimes if we aren't able to come into God's presence, because we aren't grateful or thankful?

God's word reminds us …

Sing praises to God and to his name! Sing loud praises to him who rides the clouds. His name is the LORD—rejoice in his presence! ~ Psalm 68:4 (NLT)

Come, let's shout praises to God, raise the roof for the Rock who saved us! Let's march into his presence singing praises, lifting the rafters with our hymns! ~ Psalm 95:1-2 (MSG)

"Let us come before His presence with thanksgiving; let us make a joyful noise to Him with songs of praise!" ~ Psalm 95:2 (AMP)

"On your feet now—applaud God! Bring a gift of laughter, sing yourselves into his presence." ~ Psalm 100:1-2 (MSG)

"Serve the Lord with gladness! Come before His presence with singing!" ~ Psalm 100:2 (AMP).

"He who brings an offering of praise and thanksgiving honors and glorifies Me; and he who orders his way aright [who prepares the way that I may show him], to him I will demonstrate the salvation of God." ~ Psalm 50:23 (AMP)

"Do not be anxious about anything, but in everything, by prayer and petition, with thanksgiving, present your requests to God. And the peace of God, which transcends all understanding, will guard your hearts and your minds in Christ Jesus." ~ Philippians 4:6-7 (NIV)

Heavenly Father how I praise You! Thank You for all You do, for all You are, for Your love, Your kindness, Your mercy, Your grace, Your forgiveness. Thank You, Father. I come into Your presence with joy.

"Through Him, therefore, let us constantly and at all times offer up to God a sacrifice of praise, which is the fruit of lips that thankfully acknowledge and confess and glorify His name." ~ Hebrews 13:15 (AMP)

~ Faithful Love ~

The world is hurting. Wounds raw and open. Loneliness wails in the night, and the silence deafens. Hearts barely beating, aortas desperately pump life. People fail, turn their backs, leave, and don't respond.

Yet, God's arms are open wide. He longs to heal the broken-hearted, to bind wounds. His ears are always open. His life grants life, new life, new mercies every morning. His hope, His truth, His grace, His love never fails.

You are never alone. Never without hope. Never too far from God's faithful enduring love.

"Give thanks to the Lord, for He is good! His faithful love endures forever. Give thanks to the God of gods. His faithful love endures forever. Give thanks to the Lord of lords. His faithful love endures forever. Give thanks to him who alone does mighty miracles. His faithful love endures forever.

"Give thanks to him who made the heavens so skillfully. His faithful love endures forever. Give thanks to him who placed the earth among the waters. His faithful love endures forever. Give thanks to him who made the heavenly lights—the sun to rule the day, and the moon and stars to rule the night.

"His faithful love endures forever. He remembered us in our weakness. His faithful love endures forever. He saved us from our enemies. His faithful love endures forever. He gives food to every living thing. His faithful love endures forever. Give thanks to the God of heaven. His faithful love endures forever." ~ Psalm 136: 1-9, Psalm 136: 23-26 (NLT)

The Lord will fulfill his purpose for me; your steadfast love, O Lord, endures forever. Do not forsake the work of your hands. I know and rest in confidence upon it that the Lord will maintain the cause of the afflicted, and will secure justice for the poor and needy of His believing children. Your kingdom will go on and on, and You will rule forever. The Lord will keep all His promises; He is loyal to all He has made.

Be still, and know that I am God. For I know the plans I have for you, plans for welfare and not for evil, to give you a future and a hope. And my God will supply every need of yours according to His riches in glory in Christ Jesus. For nothing is impossible with God

~ Psalm 27:10, Deuteronomy 31:8, Psalm 32:8, Psalm 34:10, Psalm 73:26, Psalm 34:19, Psalm 41:2, Exodus 14:14, Psalm 55:16, Psalm 54:4, Psalm 41:3, Psalm 34:22, Psalm 42:8, Psalm 84:11, Psalm 138:8, Psalm 140:12, Psalm 145:13, Psalm 46:10, Jeremiah 29:11, Philippians 4:19, Luke 1:37 .

~ *Who Are You Asking For Help?* ~

When we look to others—to man's wealth and provision, jobs, the government, our family, friends, our acquaintances—instead of looking to God, we will always be disappointed, angry, and often heartsick and hopeless.

Have we so quickly forgotten God's love and promises?

Even if my father and mother abandon me, the Lord will hold me close. Do not be afraid or discouraged, for the Lord will personally go ahead of you. He will be with you; He will neither fail you nor abandon you. The Lord will instruct you and teach you in the way you should go; He will counsel you with His eye upon you.

Even strong young lions sometimes go hungry, but those who trust in the Lord will lack no good thing. My flesh and my heart may fail, but God is the strength of my heart and my portion forever.

People who do what is right may have many problems, but the Lord will solve them all. The Lord will protect them and spare their life and will bless them in the land. He will not let their enemies take them. You only need to remain calm; the Lord will fight for you.

I will call on God, and the LORD will rescue me. See, God will help me; the Lord will support me. The Lord will give them strength when they are sick, and he will make them well again. The LORD will redeem those who serve Him. No one who takes refuge in Him will be condemned.

The Lord will command His loving-kindness in the daytime, and in the night His song shall be with me, a prayer to the God of my life. For the Lord God is our sun and our shield. He gives us grace and glory. The Lord will withhold no good thing from those who do what is right.

~ Love God Button ~

What if we had an "I love God" button floating above our heads? Would it burn bright like a neon sign? Or would we wear a hat or scarf to hide our identity?

On days when we get busy with life or with the problems of this world, would our button dim? Would it flicker when our thoughts became scattered? When someone cut in front of us in traffic would our button droop?

For proper maintenance, I recommend a daily dose of Bible study added with a healthy sprinkling of praise and thanksgiving.

Love God?

Keep your light burning bright!

"You are the light that gives light to the world. A city that is built on a hill cannot be hidden. And people don't hide a light under a bowl. They put it on a lampstand so the light shines for all the people in the house. In the same way, you should be a light for other people. Live so that they will see the good things you do and will praise your Father in heaven." ~ Matthew 5:14-16 (NCV)

~ Flashing Prayers ~

My nights have been rather interesting now that I've entered the hot flash phase. Yes, I do feel like a human firefly. I'll be nice and cozy in bed, or freezing, and then all the sudden a wave of heat hits like I've been placed in an industrial dryer. Oh my goodness, who knew the body could do such odd things!

Since sleep has been rather difficult, I decided to have fun with this weird phenomenon. For some reason, the flashes sometimes hit certain body parts. So the other night when my legs decided to hit 550 degrees Fahrenheit, I prayed God would use my legs and feet to walk on His paths for His purposes.

Then when the flash moved to my hands, I asked God to use my hands to bring Him glory. Then my back ignited on fire, so I prayed I wouldn't pick up any burden I shouldn't, and that I would cast all my cares on God's strong shoulders.

Now when I flash, I burst my prayers into flame.

May I challenge those of you who are going through difficulties to use your troubles as opportunities to light up your prayer life?

Flash on friends, and blaze your prayers heavenward!

When you pass through the waters, I will be with you; and when you pass through the rivers, they will not sweep over you.

When you walk through the fire, you will not be burned; the flames will not set you ablaze. Fan into flame the gift of God.

Rejoice, though now for a little while you may have had to suffer grief in all kinds of trials. These have come so that your faith—of greater worth than gold, which perishes even though refined by fire—may be proved genuine and may result in praise, glory and honor when Jesus Christ is revealed. (Isaiah 43:22, 2 Timothy 1:6, 1 Peter 1:6-7)

~ The Amazing Cycle Of Prayer ~

Prayer is an amazing and wonderful cycle. Follow the flow with me. Our prayers are like incense traveling to heaven. The Spirit intercedes, Jesus pleads for us, and God causes all things to work for good for those who love Him and are called according to His purpose. Do you see the flow?

Our prayers come before God like incense. Then, God's Holy Spirit helps our weakness; for we don't know how to pray as we should, but the Spirit intercedes for us with groanings too deep for words. And He who searches the hearts knows what the mind of the Spirit is, because He intercedes for the saints according to the will of God. For Christ Jesus died for us and was raised to life for us, and He sits in the place of honor at God's right hand, pleading for us. And we know God causes all things to work together for good to those who love God, to those who are called according to His purpose. ~ Psalm 141:2, Romans 8:26-28, 34.

Your prayers make a difference. Even on days when you wonder if anyone is listening. Even on days when you feel so small and the world's problems are so big. Even when you are all alone with no one to listen to your cries, God in Heaven hears. Each prayer of God's children is precious and delivered straight to His throne. Your prayers move through your spirit to God's Spirit, interceded by Jesus, aligning you in His perfect will and the movements of Heaven.

Heavenly Father thank You that our prayers rise to You like incense and before they reach Your heavenly ears they are filtered through Your Holy Spirit and interceded by Your wonderful Son.

~ *What If?* ~

I meet every Saturday morning to pray with a group of women called The Fellowship of the Burning Hearts. We burn with passion to hear God's heart, to know His word, know Him, and follow the leading of His Holy Spirit.

You are never too young and never too old to pray. And I wonder, what if groups started around the world? What if we prayed not only for our families, friends, and ourselves?

What if we prayed for, our city, our government, our nation, missionaries, the churches, the persecuted church, those who are with us in traffic, the business on the corner as we wait at a stoplight, those around us while we shop?

What if we prayed for the people at our workplace, our military, police, firemen, doctors, civil servants, the actors, producers, directors, and stars in Hollywood?

What if we prayed for those who are ill, those being abused, those who are abusers, those who are enslaved, those who take advantage of others, those ensnared in pornography, those trapped in false religions… the list is endless.

Does your heart burn with passion for God? Please pray.

What if <u>you</u> started a prayer group?

Will you pray?

~ Smoke Signals ~

Friends and family members are hurting and going through difficulties. I take their requests to the Father ... prayers for comfort, provision, mighty protection, peace in the middle of storms, healing, guidance, direction, and wisdom. The prayers, rising like incense, continue throughout the day and night.

We lift up our friends to God, and I imagined placing them in a hot air balloon basket and watching as they float safely heavenward.

Saturday on the way to our prayer group, God blessed me with a photo opportunity. Not two miles from where we meet to pray, a balloon hovered above a church, the cross standing out against the morning sky.

Keep the incense of your prayers rising upward to the heavens empowering God's heavenly hosts.

"May my prayer be set before you like incense; may the lifting up of my hands be like the evening sacrifice." ~ Psalm 141:2 (NIV)

~ Enough Blessings ~

We pray for God's blessings. Perhaps even pray, "God if you let me win the lottery, then I'll help others, or then I'll have more time, or then I'll…."

Why would God bless us with more, if the blessings He has given are not enough for us to be grateful?

Are we offering back our God-given blessings so He can bless us and bless others?

Are we asking for His blessings, and yet not willing to share the blessings He has already given?

Do we want blessings without being a blessing?

When will our blessings be enough?

"Give, and you will receive. You will be given much. Pressed down, shaken together, and running over, it will spill into your lap. The way you give to others is the way God will give to you." ~ Luke 6:38 (NCV)

~ Contagious ~

Flu season makes us keenly aware of the need for keeping our hands clean. However we forget as we walk through this life, we are contagious.

How are you infecting others?

Are you contaminating them with negativity and condemnation, or worries about today and the future?

Or, are you leaving the blessings of Christ's love, joy, peace, patience, kindness, goodness, faithfulness, gentleness, and self-control?

We are contagious; choose what you spread to others – gloom and doom, or life and hope.

"Finally, dear brothers and sisters, we ask you to pray for us. Pray that the Lord's message will spread rapidly and be honored wherever it goes, just as when it came to you." ~ 2 Thessalonians 3:1 (NLT)

~ Never Be ~

GOD is magnificent; He can never be praised enough. The LORD's plans stand firm forever; His intentions can never be shaken. Truly He is my rock and my salvation; He is my fortress, I will never be shaken. I tell you the truth; those who listen to my message and believe in God who sent me have eternal life. They will never be condemned for their sins, but they have already passed from death into life.

But look! I tell you this secret: We will not all sleep in death, but we will all be changed. It will take only a second—as quickly as an eye blinks—when the last trumpet sounds. The trumpet will sound, and those who have died will be raised to live forever, and we will all be changed. This body that can be destroyed must clothe itself with something that can never be destroyed. And this body that dies must clothe itself with something that can never die. So this body that can be destroyed will clothe itself with that which can never be destroyed, and this body that dies will clothe itself with that which can never die.

When this happens, this Scripture will be made true: Death is destroyed forever in victory. Death, where is your victory? Death, where is your pain?

Praise the Lord! Those who are in Christ, will never be shaken, never be moved, never be condemned, never be thirsty, never be hungry, and never be destroyed!

~ Psalm 145:3 MSG, Psalm 33:11 NLT, Psalm 62:2 NIV, John 5:24 NLT, 1 Corinthians 15:51-55 NCV

~ Winging Prayers On Praise ~

Family members and friends are currently going through major difficulties. Lives are being changed in heart-breaking situations. And even though we know God is there and still loves us, yet the worries remain about tomorrow. So we carry our cares to The One Who cares. And on knees we beg for breakthroughs and help.

I stood in the laundry room with dirty clothes at my feet, and I cried out to God–that stone hearts would be melted, little ones would be kept safe, and new paths would be opened.

And then I remembered the true-life happenings with God's people in the Bible. In 2 Chronicles 20, the Israelites faced impossible odds against a vast army. But when the people began to sing and praise the Lord, God set ambushes against their enemies.

So my prayers took wings of praise for Who God is, for what He does, for His love, for His power, for His protection, and for all that He does for His people.

God is a good God. *Always.*

No matter what is happening. No matter what has happened. No matter what the future holds. God is a good God. Wing your prayers with praise and let Him fight.

As they began to sing and praise, God set ambushes against their enemy and they were defeated. (2 Chronicles 20:21-22)

~ To Be Or Not To Be ~

I'm stymied. Stuck. My mind is scrambling through thoughts and yet way too quiet. I have blogs and emails to write, online friends to answer. I have proposals to finish. Fiction manuscripts are in progress, and instead all my characters are sitting silently in a proverbial waiting room. And my stagnant mind is whirling in place. Ack!

I want to DO!

Then I wonder, am I concentrating so hard on doing, that I'm missing being? Does God sometimes just want me TO BE–be in His presence, be His child, be with Him? What does God want me to be? And in His word I find the answers.

Be still before the Lord and wait patiently for him. Be strong and take heart and wait for the Lord. Rejoice in the Lord and be glad. Be on your guard; stand firm in the faith; be men of courage; be strong. Be merciful, just as your Father is merciful.

Be joyful in hope, patient in affliction, faithful in prayer. Be joyful always. Be holy and blameless in His sight. Be completely humble and gentle; be patient, bearing with one another in love. Be kind and compassionate to one another, forgiving each other, just as in Christ God forgave you.

Be self-controlled. Be very careful, then, how you live—not as unwise but as wise. Be strong in the Lord and in his mighty power. For in him we live and move and have our being.

Father, help me to stop trying so hard to do. Because being in Your presence is where I find the answers to every situation and every problem. Help my mind to stay focused on being with You and my heart to be set on You. May the words of my mouth and the meditation of my heart be pleasing in Your sight. Thank You Father, that I can always be with You!

~ Psalm 37:7, Psalm 27:14, Psalm 32:11, 1 Corinthians 16:13, Luke 6:36, Romans 12:12, 1 Thessalonians 15:16, Ephesians 1:4, Ephesians 4:2, Ephesians 4:32, 1 Peter 1:13, Ephesians 5:15, Ephesians 6:10, Acts 17:28.

~ Period. ~

I'll admit I have problems with punctuation. Commas should be pauses, like when I talk. Periods used when I pause longer than a pause. Period. Semicolons, colons, ellipses, question marks, exclamation points, and dashes decorated my pages at random intervals.

Grammar lovers, please don't judge me. If you see misused punctuation or grammar problems, prayers are appreciated. I have so much more to learn.

I notice we tend to punctuate life. We question God, exclaiming surely He should have done something differently. We put periods on those who suffer traumatic events, stating that no healing is available and their future is without hope. When things don't go our way, or we don't understand, we plop down a big fat period on our proverbial life pages and refuse to go forward.

We punctuate life without knowing the full sentence. Only God knows when a semicolon, exclamation point, question, colon, dash, or ellipses, is proper. With God our lives have no period – ever. Life goes on, forever.

The only period we need to concern ourselves with is that Jesus Christ brings forgiveness of sins and the promise of new life, new hope, and new beginnings. And that is the wonderful truth. Period.

Rejoice! If Jesus Christ is your Savior, the period at the end of your life's sentence becomes a dash to a wonderful, joy-filled eternity.

~ Loving The Passion ~

Prayer can and should encompass every moment of our day, regardless of our activities. Yet, prayer isn't a chore, task, or something to be checked off a to-do list. Prayer isn't rote memorization or only bringing our wants and needs.

Prayer is passion.

Prayer is connecting with the God of the universe, holy, high and exalted, who desires a relationship with each of us (me and you). Wow!

Prayer is protection, a calm in the storm of life, and a safe harbor. Prayer is sharing life's joys and difficulties with our Creator. Prayer is talking and listening. Prayer is spending time with the One who knows you best. No pretenses are needed. Prayer is an incredible, awesome opportunity to love and fully be loved.

Please don't miss an amazing moment in prayer.

Heavenly Father thank You that You want to talk with us. Thank You that You take the time, day or night, to always have a listening ear for Your children.

~ Fun And Games, Until...~

Windows down and music blaring in my teenage ears, I drove the quiet, winding, roads to my parent's home in the country. Afternoon sunshine cast playful shadows on the tree-lined blacktop, and all was right with the world.

The sound of honking drew my attention. A car moved close to my bumper then danced and swerved behind me. Inside two guys waved and smiled. Grateful for the flirting and feeling adventurous, I played a game of cat and mouse.

A few miles further down the road, their car sped up and pulled next to mine. Smiles and laughter were exchanged ... until a shotgun appeared out of the passenger side window pointed at my face.

Glancing ahead, I knew my turn approached. My car, sliding and screeching, somehow managed to take that turn on two wheels, leaving my would-be attackers barreling down the highway.

Full-speed I flew home, hid my car behind the house, watched and waited. Thankfully, I never saw them again.

Life is full of temptations and situations that seem risk-free. The "harmless" flirting, the relationship that crosses a moral line, or the gossip about a friend or family member— all seemingly small and innocuous until they blow up in our face.

Playing cat and mouse with the enemy has consequences. We may escape a large disaster, but we lose a piece of ourselves, and we lose communion with God.

God offers forgiveness for wayward ways. However, we are left with regrets, broken relationships, and broken trust. The pain and sting may leave, but memories linger.

Don't smile and wave at the enemy, run for the safety, protection, and covering of God's truth.

"The highway of the upright avoids evil; the one who guards his way protects his life." ~ Proverbs 16:17 (HCSB)

~ *Stop, Drop, And Roll* ~

Are you weary? Has life beaten you bloody? Can you see nothing good? Are you feeling hopeless, deserted, and without joy?

Stop
Stop and remember God's truth – God loves you and His love never fails.
He won't desert you or forsake you. You are forever safe in Him.

Drop
Drop your fears, worries, and life's heartaches at the feet of Jesus.
Jesus is eternal hope and joy.

Roll
Roll your burdens on God's strong shoulders.
Nothing is impossible for Him.

Heavenly Father when life is so very hard, **help me to stop, drop, and roll into Your strong arms.**

~ Declaring Freedom ~

Do you want to be free and unchained and unhindered by life? Believing in Jesus Christ results in amazing, incredible, eternal freedom.

Without Jesus Christ, life is unsettled, unaware, uncertain, unclean, uncomfortable, undecided, undefined, unfaithful, unfortunate, unfruitful, ungodly, unhappy, unjustifiable, undisciplined, unprotected, unrighteous, and we become unbelieving unbelievers.

In Jesus Christ, we are settled, aware, certain, clean, comfortable, decided, defined, faithful, fortunate, fruitful, Godly, happy, justifiable, disciplined, protected, righteous, and we become a believing believer.

We are set free through Christ! In Jesus we are unchained, unbound, unbroken, unburdened, undamaged, undefiled, unblemished, unspotted, unashamed, uninhibited, undaunted, understood, unimpeded, unperturbed, untroubled, undismayed, undying, to live unending with our unfailing Savior.

Jesus said, "The Spirit of the Lord is on Me, because He has anointed Me to preach good news to the poor. He has sent Me to proclaim freedom to the captives and recovery of sight to the blind, to set free the oppressed, to proclaim the year of the Lord's favor." ~ Luke 4:18-19 (HCSB)

"The Scriptures declare that we are all prisoners of sin, so we receive God's promise of freedom only by believing in Jesus Christ." ~ Galatians 3:22 (NLT)

"God sent him to buy freedom for us who were slaves to the law, so that he could adopt us as his very own children" ~ Galatians 4:5 (NLT)

"He is so rich in kindness and grace that he purchased our freedom with the blood of his Son and forgave our sins." ~ Ephesians 1:7 (NLT)

"In Christ we can come before God with freedom and without fear. We can do this through faith in Christ." ~ Ephesians 3:12 (NCV)

"That Holy Spirit is the guarantee that we will receive what God promised for his people until God gives **full freedom** to those who are his—to bring praise to God's glory." ~ Ephesians 1:14 (NCV)

"For the Lord is the Spirit, and wherever the Spirit of the Lord is, there is freedom." ~ 2 Corinthians 3:17 (NLT)

"If you **declare** with your mouth, 'Jesus is Lord,' and if you believe in your heart that God raised Jesus from the dead, you will be saved. We believe with our hearts, and so we are made right with God. And we declare with our mouths that we believe, and so we are saved. As the Scripture says, '

"Anyone who trusts in him will never be disappointed.' That Scripture says 'anyone' because there is no difference between those who are Jews and those who are not. The same Lord is the Lord of all and gives many blessings to all who trust in him, as the Scripture says, 'Anyone who calls on the Lord will be saved.'" ~ Romans 10:9-13 (NCV)

"So if the Son makes you free, you will be truly free." ~ John 8:36 (NCV)

Will you join me by declaring your freedom?

~ Hidden In His Presence ~

During a time of prayer, I came across two versions of the same verse.

"For he will conceal me there when troubles come; he will hide me in his sanctuary. He will place me out of reach on a high rock." ~ Psalm 27:4-5 (NLT)

"For in the day of trouble he will keep me safe in his dwelling; he will hide me in the shelter of his tabernacle and set me high upon a rock." ~ Psalm 27:5 (NIV)

The words soothe my soul. And when I went deeper by looking through the Greek, Hebrew, and Webster's 1828 dictionary definitions of key words, I was thrilled at the marvelous promises this verse gives.

Keep safe – hide, conceal, store up, to be **treasured, be cherished**, to be stored up.

Hide – conceal, store up, to be treasured, be **cherished**, to be stored up.

Conceal – To withhold from sight, to conceal, and to **heal**; the primary sense is to strain, hold, stop, restrain, make fast or strong, To **keep close** or secret.

Trouble - The primary sense is to turn or to stir, to whirl about, as in L. turbo, turbinis, a **whirlwind**. Hence the sense of **agitation, disturbance**.

Dwelling – covering, dwelling (of human or lion), **inhabiting**; residing; sojourning; continuing with fixed attention. Habitation; place of residence; abode.

Shelter – **hiding place**, secret place, shelter, covering, veil, secretly, in secret.

Sanctuary – **A sacred place**; particularly among the Israelites, the most retired part of the temple at Jerusalem, called the Holy of Holies, in which was kept the ark of the covenant, and into which no person was permitted to enter except the high priest, and that only once a year to intercede for the people. A **place of protection**; a sacred asylum. Hence a sanctuary-man is one that resorts to a sanctuary for protection. Shelter; protection.

Tabernacle – **home**, dwelling place, a permanent dwelling.

Set high – **raise up**, present (an offering).

Rock – a title of God, with a focus of stability, and possibly as a place of security and safety In Scripture, figuratively, defense; means of **safety; protection**; strength; asylum. Firmness; a firm or immovable foundation.

How precious that when trouble whirlwinds, agitates and disturbs, our Heavenly Father cherishes, conceals, heals and safely covers us in the secret place of His love.

~ The Real Story – Starring You! ~

I'm walking a tad taller today, and looking at life a little differently. Between our pastor's sermon on Hebrews 12:1-3, regarding running the race, and John Eldredge's, awesome book and DVD, *Epic: The Story God Is Telling,* I've realized some really cool things.

In the past when I considered the "race" we were to run, I thought I needed to be better, faster, and stronger than other competitors.

However I've learned I'm not running against others, I'm running a race specifically designed for me. And that race will never have an obstacle or difficulty that God won't be there with a rescue or to provide the grace and strength needed to fulfill the ultimate goal.

As a writer, every character placed in my stories, every scene and word chosen, has a purpose. In the same way, before we were born, The Author of the universe, The One who loves with an unfailing love, designed and created us to be cast in the starring role of our story.

Through the highs, lows, heartaches, and joys we were created for an epic adventure. We can choose detours. We can even decide we don't want to follow God. And even if we do follow God, the enemy will taunt us with problems, illness, failure, weakness, heartache, and tragedy. However God is there with solutions, healing, grace, restoration, strength, peace, and comfort. We are never alone.

And, the best part? For those who chose Christ, the ending will be wonderful—an unchangeable ending where good always wins, culminating in a happily-ever-after.

So guess what, you are a star!

You, the one and only you, have been chosen to play you. Take a bow or curtsy, my friend, your Heavenly Father cast you in the lead role!

~ Freely Free ~

All have sinned, all fallen short of the glory of God. Yet when you repent and ask for forgiveness, God is there with open arms. His forgiveness is complete. Your sin is erased from His memory. He won't continue punishing you for what He can't remember. And God doesn't lie, that is His promise and that is the truth.

As Jesus said to the women caught in adultery, "Then Jesus stood up again and said to the woman, 'Where are your accusers? Didn't even one of them condemn you?' 'No, Lord,' she said. And Jesus said, 'Neither do I. Go and sin no more.'" ~ John 8:10-11 (NLT)

Don't let Satan continue to accuse you. Don't live under the lie of the enemy that you can't be forgiven or that God continues to condemn you.

"Now there is no condemnation for those who belong to Christ Jesus. And because you belong to him, the power of the life-giving Spirit has freed you from the power of sin that leads to death. So if the Son sets you free, you are truly free." ~ Romans 8:1-2, John 8:36 (NLT.)

You have been set free to live freely in Christ's freedom. Freely live free in Christ!

~ Seeing the Unseen ~

"For our present troubles are small and won't last very long. Yet they produce for us a glory that vastly outweighs them and will last forever! So we don't look at the troubles we can see now; rather, we fix our gaze on things that cannot be seen. For the things we see now will soon be gone, but the things we cannot see will last forever." ~ 2 Corinthians 4:17-18 (NLT)

No matter how long you live, life here is temporary. We forget we are only passing through. Why do we focus on things that will not last, things that won't remain, people who are only blips on the radar screen of eternity? Why do we only see what we can see? Oh there is so much more. So much more. Eternally more.

Those who believe in Christ are given eternal life (John 3:16-17).

In Christ we forgo judgment through His grace (John 5:24, Romans 6:23)

In Christ we are raised into eternal life, given new bodies, in the eternity of heaven (2 Corinthians 5:1, John 6:40)

In Christ, we are promised eternal soul-safety and no one can snatch us out of His hand (John 10:28)

In Christ, we have an eternal home prepared just for us (John 14:2, Psalm 23:6)

With God, we have joy-forever (Psalm 16:11

Oh the joy of the unseen is the past erased through the forgiveness, grace, and mercy of Jesus Christ to the fullness of new life and eternal new beginnings.

Do you see the unseen? For now we see only dimly, but when we are face-to-face with our God, we will know as we are fully known. (1 Corinthians 13:12)

~ For I Know The Plans ~

I love researching and studying the meanings of words using the Bible, Webster's dictionary, Bible study references, and Greek and Hebrew definitions. Here is a fun examination of one of my favorite verses, Jeremiah 29:11.

"'For I know the plans I have for you,' declares the Lord, 'plans to prosper you and not to harm you, plans to give you hope and a future.'" ~ Jeremiah 29:11 (NIV)

"'For I know the plans I have for you,' says the Lord. 'They are plans for good and not for disaster, to give you a future and a hope.'" ~ Jeremiah 29:11 (NLT)

"'For I know the thoughts and plans that I have for you,' says the Lord, 'thoughts and plans for welfare and peace and not for evil, to give you hope in your final outcome.'" ~ Jeremiah 29:11 (AMP)

Some of the definitions are:

Plans = Thought, design, purpose, to determine. A series of steps to be carried out or goals to be accomplished

Prosper = Peace, safety, prosperity, well-being, intactness, wholeness. Peace can have a focus of security, safety which can bring feelings of satisfaction, well-being, and contentment

Hope = The general feeling that some desire will be fulfilled. Expect with desire.

God has a design. He knows the steps that need to be taken to carry out the ultimate goal for our lives. His plan is good, peaceful, safe, prosperous, leads to well-being, wholeness, and contentment. His plan is not evil, harmful or disastrous. His plan gives a desirous expectation in our final, future outcome.

Isn't that neat? There are treasures just waiting to be found. Pray and ask for understanding, dive deeper with God and His word, and enjoy the amazing depths of His plan, purpose, and love.

~ Who Is He? ~

In church we watched a video in which people were asked, "Who is Jesus?"

Many answers saddened me, but all made me think.

Who is Jesus to *me*? He is my Savior, my friend, and the Lord of my life.

I don't answer lightly, nor because I was raised in the Christian church. My answer is based on personally discovering a love beyond earthly constraints.

My life has not been without hardships, I haven't lived in a bubble, and I am not one to blindly follow. Through the highs and lows of my journey, I have seen the hand of God – whether protecting, pulling me through, calling me back, or leading me home. I am drawn to His grace, mercy, desire for the hurting and lost, and His unfailing love.

> I love a God who loves me.
> I love a God who loves you.
> Who is Jesus to you?
> Personally?

Life is offered – here and now – and eternally. **Who is Jesus to you?**

"I tell you the truth, those who listen to my message and believe in God who sent me have eternal life. They will never be condemned for their sins, but they have already passed from death into life." ~ John 5:24 (NLT)

~ Searching For Truth ~

There are so many hurting people, so much violence, trauma, and heartaches. Reality almost overwhelms me. I want to take away world hunger and stop the wars. I want to fix everyone's problems, take away the hurts, and help those without Jesus find Him. I'll be honest I think I would curl into a fetal position if the solution was only through me.

Fortunately, during my Bible study time I came across these verses to help me get back my prospective.

"You began your life in Christ by the Spirit. Now are you trying to make it completely your own power? That is foolish. ... You will not succeed by your own strength or power but by my Spirit, says the Lord All-Powerful." ~ Galatians 3:3, Zechariah 4:6 (NLT)

I can't do anything without God. I can't make it a moment without Him to guide me. I can't fix the world, but I can rest in The One who can. The only way I can stand firm is to remember God's truths found in His words.

God promises - I will search for the lost and bring back the strays. I will bind up the injured and strengthen the weak ... God our Savior, who wants all men to be saved and to come to a knowledge of the truth. For there is one God and one mediator between God and men, the man Christ Jesus, who gave himself as a ransom for all men—the testimony given in its proper time. (Ezekiel 34:16, 1 Timothy 2:3-6)

God delivers - The angel of the LORD encamps around those who fear Him, and He delivers them. The LORD helps them and delivers them; He delivers them from the wicked and saves them, because they take refuge in Him. He fulfills the desires of those who fear Him; He hears their cry and saves them." (Psalm 34:7, Psalm 37:40, Psalm 145:19)

God watches and listens - Evening, morning and noon I cry out in distress, and He hears my voice. The eyes of the Lord are on the righteous and His ears are attentive to their cry. To the LORD I cry aloud, and He answers me from His holy hill. (Psalm 55:17, Psalm 34:15, Psalm 3:4)

God heals -. He heals the brokenhearted and binds up their wounds. Praise the LORD, O my soul, and forget not all his benefits—who forgives all your sins and heals all your diseases." (Psalm 147:3, Psalm 103:2-3)

God is our refuge -. The LORD is a refuge for the oppressed, a stronghold in times of trouble. Those who dwell in the shelter of the Most High will rest in the shadow of the Almighty. He will cover you with His feathers, and under His wings you will find refuge; His faithfulness will be your shield and rampart." (Psalm 9:9, Psalm 91:1, 4)

God is our rest – Jesus invites us to come to Him, those who are weary and burdened, and He will give us rest. Take His yoke upon you and learn from Him, for He is gentle and humble in heart, and you will find rest for your souls. For His yoke is easy and His burden is light. Our souls finds rest in God alone; our salvation comes from Him. (Matthew 11:28-30, Psalm 62:1)

God is our victor – Jesus tells us things, so that in Him we have peace. In this world we will have trouble. But take heart! He has overcome the world. He will wipe every tear from their eyes. There will be no more death or mourning or crying or pain, for the old order of things has passed away. He who was seated on the throne said, "I am making everything new!" (John 16:33, Revelation 21:4-5)

Heavenly Father, thank You for Your Truth. Thank You that for every need, every fear or worry, Your Truth provides guidance, direction, and comfort.

~ Oh My, What An Awesome God! ~

With each passing year, through the highs and lows of life, I've grown to love God deeper as I've experienced the different facets of His personality. This devotion contains only a snippet of the verses that describe our great, loving, and mighty God. God loves **you**!!!!

Oh my, what an awesome God!

Study God's word. Underline verses that give you hope and bring you closer to His heart. The author of life is waiting to speak to you.

Our God is strength, our rock, fortress, and deliverer. He is powerful, a warrior, greater than all other gods. He is a shield for all who take refuge in Him, a refuge for the oppressed, a stronghold in times of trouble. He is our shepherd. He is our light. The Lord is our banner. He is with us.

The Lord is peace and our helper. He is good, faithful, and just. He is slow to anger, abounding in love and forgiving sin and rebellion. He keeps His covenant of love to a thousand generations of those who love Him and keep His commands. The word of the Lord is flawless.

The law of the Lord is perfect, reviving the soul. For the word of the Lord is right and true; He is faithful in all He does. The Lord is not slow in keeping His promise…. He is patient with you, not wanting anyone to perish, but everyone to come to repentance. For this God is our God forever and ever; He will be our guide even to the end.

What are your favorite verses?

We truly do have an awesome God!

~ Freeway Christianity ~

I don't want freeway Christianity with breakneck speeds, over the shoulder prayers, and busyness of life that keeps my eyes on the world and off God's sufficiency. I want to dive deep in His word and mine the treasure of truths waiting to be discovered. I want to sing His praises. I want to study the additional facets radiating from my Savior when I meet those who love and serve Him. I long to point the lost to The One who brings salvation, hope, and healing.

And when hard times come and difficulties arise, I want to praise Him in the storms. I don't want to waste a moment of time with my Savior and God. I want His total, encompassing presence.

I want to grow and learn each day, steeping within Him. I want to feel, touch, and experience life in the fullest for His glory.

Oh precious Father, help me to live every moment in the moment. Make me wholly Yours.

What kind of Christian do you hope to be?

"One thing I ask of the LORD, this is what I seek: that I may dwell in the house of the LORD all the days of my life, to gaze upon the beauty of the LORD and to seek Him in His temple." ~ Psalm 27:4 (NIV)

~ Spring Blessings ~

Winter gray and cold days threaten to stifle our joy, but God always brings the Spring. And that which seems to be dead, comes back to life. Seeds devoid of life, morph into new buds promising life does continue after death.

I love Spring! Tiny purple flowers, red bud trees puffed out in fuchsia, daylilies stretch their limbs from underneath the mulch, and Bradford pear trees shed cotton white flowers for soft green leaves. Every moment, a new shade of green, a new leaf, or a new bud sprouts as the browns of winter fade into the vibrant colors of spring.

For the sake of my neighbors, I stifle the urge to break into song. But my soul will not be silenced.

How grateful I am for a God who thaws the winter cold for the warmth of spring and adorns the plants for our enjoyment.

Dear Heavenly Father, open my eyes to see the wonders You have created. Help me to be like the little child who stops and marvels over the intricacies of everything around them.

Fully engage me to see the treasures You give us each day. You've stolen my heart. Thank You for spoiling me again today.

I ask these things in the precious Name of Your Son, Jesus Christ, who is my Savior. Amen

~ Deep Calls ~

Because of God's deep love we are saved. Worship Him with deep awe and respect.

Seek His deep truths. Like a submarine diving deep into the depths of God's word, where His light and truth shine the way.

Dive deep. To go deeper you can't keep focusing on the surface issues of life. Don't keep floundering in temptations, fears, and worries.

Deeply desire a deep friendship with God to deeply desire His desires.

Run silent, where only the sound of His voice whispers in your spirit.

Experience deep joy by staying in the fullness of God's joy.

Live in God's deep, high, and wide love … for in His love we deeply love.

"The LORD reached down from above and took me; he pulled me from the deep water." ~ Psalm 18:16 (NCV)

~ Accepting Love's Perfect Gift ~

The Christmas season is celebrated with decorations inside and outside homes. Traffic swells around shopping centers. Malls and stores are filled with trinkets and items to purchase. Grocery shelves are lined with goodies to entice and tempt. Credit cards are over-used and over-burdened. Faces are etched with worry trying to find that perfect gift.

And yet in the manger, waits The One who came to bring soul peace. The One who is The Way, The Truth, and The Life. The One who beckons stillness, burden lifting, and grace. The One who brings treasures from heaven offering forgiveness, rest, and restoration. Jesus Christ, birthed from love, the embodiment of love, holds arms wide open offering love's perfect gift.

Love's perfect gift isn't just for Christmas; Jesus offers forgiveness, grace, and mercy every day of the year.

Will you accept The perfect gift of love?

Heavenly Father thank You for the news of great joy the angels brought the shepherds at the birth of Your Son. Thank You for Jesus. Thank You that You love us enough to send Your Son. Jesus thank You that You came to save us. Thank You for the amazing gift of Your salvation!

(See Luke 2:10-11, John 3:16-17)

~ *Please Come Out To Play* ~

My heart is heavy. Not for myself, but for those who I know are afraid. They've been hurt in the past, and the memory is still too strong to trust. They peek out from behind walls they built to help them survive.

Every now and then I see the little girl or little boy who lives in the adult, venture to come out to laugh and play, who desires to trust once more. And I long to wrap them in God's love and show them He is safe.

God will never leave you or forsake you. He won't take advantage of you. He will never, ever be two-faced, mean, or cruel. He won't talk bad about you to others. He sent His Son, Jesus to show you the way home, the way to safety.

God is perfect, this world is not. Even those who claim to be His children can be cruel, petty, and mean. And there are those who claim to be His, but they are not. They only use His name for their own purposes. Please don't judge God by the failures of man.

God's hands are open and safe. He can help you break down the barriers of fear, self protection, and self-reliance, to freedom in Christ.

And as you allow God the freedom to move in your heart, His joy, peace, and love, expands and grows. Please come out to play.

Heavenly Father I pray for my friend. I pray they will come out to play in the beauty, joy, and eternal safety of Your love.

"Trust in, lean on, rely on, and have confidence in Him at all times, you people; pour out your hearts before Him. God is a refuge for us (a fortress and a high tower). Selah [pause, and calmly think of that]!" ~ Psalm 62:8 (AMP)

~ Cherished ~

Cherish — To treat with tenderness and affection; to give warmth, ease or comfort to. To hold as dear; to embrace with affection; to foster, and encourage. To treat in a manner to encourage growth, by protection, aid, attendance, or supplying nourishment.

I want to be cherished-embraced with tenderness and affection, held dear, protected, nourished, and comforted. I want to be safe, heart safe.

While grocery shopping, I watched people. I wondered if they felt cherished. I noticed those with sad eyes and wanted to wrap them in God's love, because God's love is a cherishing love.

My sweet husband cherishes and loves me, and I cherish and love him, but God's love is the one place our hearts will always be kept eternally safe. Life here on planet earth is hard. Evil and illness exists, death happens to us all. But God's love is unending, faithful, and forever.

And with God's love you are always, always cherished.

Yet I wonder, am I truly cherishing the love God so freely bestows?

Heavenly Father, thank You for Your cherishing love. Oh that I may always cherish You!

~ Ripple On ~

Everything you do for the Kingdom has a purpose and fruit that lasts forever.

Every life you have touched, every seed planted for God's Kingdom has a ripple effect. The one person you talked to or ministered to in God's name, passes on that blessing to others, and it ripples throughout the ages.

Every prayer is not constrained by time or place or earthly constraints, your prayers ripple throughout eternity.

And the Heavenly rewards we receive continue to ripple forever.

Whatever you do, whatever you say, however you pray, ripple on, dear friends!

Heavenly Father I want to make ripples and splashes for eternity. Let my little ripples ripple mightily for You!

~ Spurred On ~

*"And let us consider how we may **spur one another on toward love and good deeds**. Let us not give up meeting together, as some are in the habit of doing, but let us encourage one another—and all the more as you see the Day approaching"*
~ Hebrews 10:24-25 (NIV)

When we gather as friends, when we gather as brothers and sisters in Christ, we are to encourage and build up the body. It's so easy to complain about our situation or the situation the world is in. But as Christians, Christ followers, we are to do all for the glory of God without complaining.

And if we have a heavenly perspective the daily problems lose their foothold. Jesus didn't come to overthrow Caesar; He came to set captives free from earthly bondage that comes from the enemy.

It's so easy to look at our government, health care, rising inflation and lose hope. But if we look to God who promises to provide all our needs, it doesn't matter who is in charge of the government or healthcare or the rate of inflation.

When we study God's word, truly study and dig, we find His truths and we tap into the living water. The water that provides nourishment for us and others so that we don't live in fear and we continue to bear fruit. Because we know who we trust, and our trust is firmly planted in God's truth. Nothing is impossible for Him. Nothing is too hard for Him. Nothing can stand against Him. And as His children we are always and eternally safe.

Heavenly Father help spur me on so that I may spur others on to Your truth, hope, and joy.

"Therefore go and make disciples of all nations, baptizing them in the name of the Father and of the Son and of the Holy Spirit, and teaching them to obey everything I have commanded you. And surely I am with you always, to the very end of the age." ~ Matthew 28:19-20 (NIV)

~ The Master Plan ~

We've built several homes and worked with an architect. Once the plans were drawn and finalized, a builder was contracted to do the work. During the building process problems were always encountered. Perhaps something was left out, or something put in the wrong place, or mistakes made, or the scheduling went haywire. During all that, the master plan never changed.

God has an incredible plan for you. Before you were born, He designed you for a divine, amazing purpose no one else on this earth can fulfill but you. You've been called for a holy calling, not according to your works, but according to His purpose.

No matter what happened in the past, no matter what will happen today and in the future. Nothing can change God's Master Plan.

Heavenly Father thank You that Your plans never fail, and Your plans for me are always good. And even when mistakes are made or the enemy attacks, thank You Father that Your wonderful master plan never changes.

~ Never Letting Go ~

She sat on the side of the road, tears staining her cheeks, exhausted, alone, not a friend in the world. Oblivious to her agony, cars whizzed past stirring the heat. A few steps and it would all be over. The nightmares would end, her shattered heart would cease to beat, and the pain would end.

Rising to her feet she took a step forward. "Where are you God? If you exist, why did you allow this never-ending suffering?"

Feeling a presence, she stopped, looked, but she was alone. Always alone. And yet her legs wouldn't move, seemingly glued to the gravel of the shoulder only a foot from the road. The whoosh of air with each car and truck whipped her hair, dust stinging her eyes.

She turned her head upward. "How can you know the pain I feel? Let me go!"

I love you.

The gentle voice shook to her inner core. Again she could see no one. But she knew what she heard. "If it's you … if you're real … tell me again."

I love you.

Sobs wracked her body, and there by the side of the road, the words whether in her soul or audible told her she was loved. Loved by the God of the universe, who knows what it's like to be abandoned, hated, humiliated, falsely accused, beaten, tortured, mocked, stripped of everything and everyone they loved on earth.

In that moment she knew forever, He would never let her go.

Wherever you are, whatever you've done, whatever has been done to you, God's love will never let you go.

Don't give up, God will never give up on you. He loves you.

God's word promises, I have loved you with an unfailing love. (Jeremiah 31:3)

God's love never lets go and never fails.

~ Strapped In Tight, Expecting Great Things! ~

I believe God hears and answers prayers, but have I been expecting great things from a great God?

Unfortunately doubt rears its ugly, little matted head and responds, "Well who are you to bother God? You probably shouldn't even ask, He's probably busy. He might not do that, or maybe God will do a small thing, or just a little thing."

I need to stomp down that thinking. I am God's child. The God, Great and Mighty God, blows my socks off time and time again with the amazing, wonderful things He does.

Why on earth have I limited God with my unbelief or my earthly viewpoint?

God's mere breath brings life. His words create the universe. He parts seas, stops the sun in place, calms the seas, and conquers sin and death.

Nothing is impossible for God. We should expect great things from a great God! And as His children, never limit how He wants to move.

Dear Heavenly Father, forgive me for limiting my thoughts, my prayers, and my view of Your magnificence. Help me to turn my eyes and heart back on You and You alone.

Oh Precious Father, thank You for who You are and for all You do. I'm strapping in tight for a fun, amazing, wild ride, for You are the God of great things! I love You Forever, Father!

"Now to Him Who, by (in consequence of) the [action of His] power that is at work within us, is able to [carry out His purpose and] do superabundantly, far over and above all that we [dare] ask or think [infinitely beyond our highest prayers, desires, thoughts, hopes, or dreams]—To Him be glory in the church and in Christ Jesus throughout all generations forever and ever. Amen (so be it)." ~ Ephesians 3:20-21 (AMP)

~ Parched ~

Dragging and stumbling across a weary wasteland. Troubles, doubts, worries, and fears, afflict and pummel. Violence and turmoil clog the arteries of the nightly news. The world seems hopeless and dark. Parched.

Are you soul parched? Thirsty for truth? Looking for light? Hungry for hope?

Jesus is the answer.

The way is lit by The Way. Truth is discovered through The Truth. Life is found in The Life. True joy, true hope, and eternal peace come through the grace of Jesus Christ. Jesus is the answer. Soul parched lives are eternally quenched by The Living Water.

Jesus is the way, the truth, and the life. He is the only way to the Father. He is the bread of life for those who are soul-hungry.

Jesus is the eternal living water to thirsty souls. Our hearts bursting with the flow of His living water.

Jesus is the light of the world and when we walk with Him we never walk in darkness, because we have the light of life.

Jesus is the one who gives peace. In Him we don't have to be troubled or afraid. When we obey Him, we remain in His love. And in the joy of Jesus we are given the fullest joy possible.

~ John 14:6, John 6:35, John 8:12, John 7:38, John 14:27, John 15:10-11

~ I Don't Want To Be A Zombie ~

I don't want to walk through life with dead flesh. I don't want to go around moaning, complaining, and attacking others. Failing and falling flesh is not a pretty thing. Even if we apply every skin cream known to man and dress up the outer layer with expensive clothes, the fact remains the epidermis is not eternal.

And the more we try to hold on to the temporary, the more miserable we become.

I want to slough off this outer, decaying body and die to self. For in self-dying and self-sacrifice, giving our all to Christ, we find internal renewing and eternal joy.

Woo hoo! In Jesus Christ, we are zombie free!

"Even though on the outside it often looks like things are falling apart on us, on the inside, where God is making new life, not a day goes by without his unfolding grace … There's far more here than meets the eye. The things we see now are here today, gone tomorrow. But the things we can't see now will last forever." ~ 2 Corinthians 4:16-18 (MSG)

"Jesus, calling the crowd to join his disciples, he said, 'Anyone who intends to come with me has to let me lead. You're not in the driver's seat; I am. Don't run from suffering; embrace it. Follow me and I'll show you how. Self-help is no help at all. Self-sacrifice is the way, my way, to saving yourself, your true self. What good would it do to get everything you want and lose you, the real you? What could you ever trade your soul for?'" ~ Mark 8:34-37 (MSG)

"I have been crucified with Christ; and it is no longer I who live, but Christ lives in me; and the life which I now live in the flesh I live by faith in the Son of God, who loved me and gave Himself up for me." ~ Galatians 2:20 (NASB)

"My flesh and my heart may fail, but God is the strength of my heart and my portion forever." ~ Psalm 73:26 (NASB)

~ Deep Water ~

"When he had finished speaking, he said to Simon, 'Put out into deep water, and let down the nets for a catch.' Simon answered, 'Master, we've worked hard all night and haven't caught anything. But because you say so, I will let down the nets.'"
~ Luke 5:4-5 (NIV)

This verse caught my attention. When Jesus says to go deep, I want to go deep. However I often stubbornly try to do things my way. I'm so busy trying to figure out the hows, whys, and whats, I can't dive deep with God.

I may be in the water, but I'm hanging onto every floatation device known to man. An elephant could sit on my back, and I'd still float. I need to rid any preconceived notions of how God will move in my life and the lives of others.

God's thoughts are not like our thoughts, His ways are higher. He knows everything in the past, present, and future. Even Simon didn't believe at that moment, but he was obedient.

That's it! All we have to do is be obedient to follow God's commands and leadings.

And in the obedience, we experience the mighty depths of His presence. Woo hoo, swimming with our Savior! We couldn't be in a better place.

Dive deep my friends, the living water is mighty fine.

Heavenly Father, help me to always be obedient and plunge into the deep water of You.

~ *Digging For Treasure* ~

Bible study isn't just about checking off we've read a verse or chapter. Bible study is digging and tunneling to find treasure in God's word, it is the unearthing of true riches, not just for us, but to share with others. Bible study is finding the treasure of God's heart.

Heavenly Father, help me not be satisfied with skimming the surface. I want to dig deep, gathering wealth and jewels of Your truth, love, grace, and mercy to share with a lost and hurting world. Help me to burrow straight to the treasure of Your heart!

~ Peace In The Battleground ~

"They cried out to the Lord in their trouble, and He brought them out of their distress. He stilled the storm to a whisper; the waves of the sea were hushed. They were glad when it grew calm, and He guided them to their desired haven."
~ Psalm 107:28-30 (NIV)

Emotions, circumstances, and situations toss and blast through our lives, leaving us shell-shocked. Where is hope? How can we be hopeful when the world around is collapsing? When the doctor calls, the bills are overdue, the children are a lost mess, and the world is a battleground?

There are days I just want to crawl into my Heavenly Father's arms and let Him tell me everything will be okay. And then His truth reminds me, one way or another, we will be okay, because we have a God that with a whisper can calm any storm. It will be okay.

Even when life is full of pain and suffering, one thing never changes and always remains—God is still God, and He is a good God.

God is eternal. God is love. He remains in control, He is just and righteous.

God's truth remains forever. He is The Great Physician and The Healer. He is the lover of our souls.

Through Him, our help and answers will come. He will never leave us or forsake us. He covers us, and under His wings we find refuge. He provides for our every need.

God's love never fails. His mercies never end. His grace covers all. No matter what happens in this world or in the battles of life, we can rest in His eternal peace.

Heavenly Father You are peace and when the battles of life come, we can rest in the knowledge that You will bring us safely home. We are eternally secure, and You have won the final battle.

~ Blessed To Bless ~

In the early 1970's two members of the oldest Sunday school class at Tallowood Baptist Church decided they wanted to help Boy's Country, a Christian home for boys.

Mrs. Chapman and Mrs. Hadlow had both been missionaries in their younger days. Even though they were widows living on limited income, they approached their church asking for donations for a benefit garage sale. For those like themselves with little resources, they divided plants in pots on their porches or in their yards to sell to other gardeners.

Armed with faith and their money, they drove to one of the large ranches near Houston. The manager took one look at their funds, declined their offer to make up the shortfall with monthly payments of $30.00, and sent them down the road.

The women were not deterred. They drove to the next ranch, and again approached the foreman. Mrs. Chapman and Mrs. Hadlow told the man they wanted to buy cows to start a herd for the children's home. And they just didn't want any bovine; they wanted the best— registered Santa Gertrudis. And they wanted female cows that already had a calf and were again expecting. Being southern ladies of delicate taste they would not ever mention the words "pregnant" or "bred".

The manager, with a smile and chuckle, called for a roundup, and the cowboys paraded the finest of their herd by the ladies. The man later said he had never seen more loving people wanting to help others. Going above and beyond the women's funds, and without requiring additional compensation, the ranch manager delivered several expecting cows and their calves to the boy's home.

Because of these women, a good-sized herd was established, providing beef, opportunities for the boys to learn ranch management, meat cutting, and caring for animals.

Two precious women, big faith, blessed to bless by an awesome God!

~ Ordinary People — Awesome God ~

Life is hard. News and negativity spreads turmoil and hopelessness. Many of my Christian friends are bogged down and discouraged, and I'll admit to occasionally joining them in those feelings. I've been stymied, stumped, and rather frustrated.

Paul reminds us to, "encourage one another and build each other up"(1 Thessalonians 5:11). When I remember how God takes ordinary people and uses them in awesome ways, my confidence grows and my soul is nourished. God's plans are never thwarted. God's goodness never ceases, and His love is unfailing. Nothing is ordinary in His Hands.

The Bible is full of examples – a shepherd boy becomes King, a harlot listed in the lineage of the King of Kings. Ordinary fisherman turned into evangelists. The list goes on and on of typical, everyday people who become extraordinary through God's touch.

God continues to work. Whether in the background or in the limelight, people are accomplishing incredible things and making ripples in eternity.

Let's spread the good news. Let's encourage one another. Let's remember and see what God does and is doing. "Remember the wonders he has done, his miracles, and the judgments he pronounced"(Psalm 105:5).

Let's share with a hurting world how God turns ordinary into awesome. No matter who you are or your level of education, when you've been with Jesus, people will notice!

"The members of the council were amazed when they saw the boldness of Peter and John, for they could see that they were ordinary men with no special training in the Scriptures. They also recognized them as men who had been with Jesus." ~ Acts 4:13 (NLT)

~ The Power of Past Prayers ~

While searching through old files, I came across a prayer I had written to God. The year was 2004, and my prayer was interspersed with scripture.

I read the prayer and was amazed. So many requests were made, and so many prayers answered.

My mountain prayer 2/18/04

"I lift up my eyes to the hills — where does my help come from? My help comes from the LORD, the Maker of heaven and earth. He will not let your foot slip — He who watches over you will not slumber; indeed, He who watches over Israel will neither slumber nor sleep. The LORD watches over you — the LORD is your shade at your right hand; the sun will not harm you by day, nor the moon by night. The LORD will keep you from all harm — he will watch over your life; the LORD will watch over your coming and going both now and forevermore." ~ Psalm 121:1-8

Oh how I long for the mountains and hills; to see the vistas of tree lined mountains in the distance, to hear the running streams and the wind through the trees, the sunlight streaming through the leaves to kiss the earth. Sit with me on the porch as we admire the works of Your hands. Let me hear the laughter of my son as he plays in the stream and runs in the hills.

"Then the LORD said, 'There is a place near me where you may stand on a rock. When my glory passes by, I will put you in a cleft in the rock and cover you with my hand until I have passed by.'" ~ Exodus 33:21-22

How my soul longs to stand in the cleft of the rock as God's glory passes by. Oh that I may feel Your presence sweet Lord. Father, cover me with Your hand. Let me stand near You.

"For the LORD your God is bringing you into a good land—a land with streams and pools of water, with springs flowing in the valleys and hills." ~ Deuteronomy 8:7

"The mountains will bring prosperity to the people, the hills the fruit of righteousness." ~ Psalm 72:3

Dear Father, any prosperity that comes into our hands let it flow out to help others, to further Your kingdom.

"The mountains skipped like rams, the hills like lambs." ~ Psalm 114:4

"He tends His flock like a shepherd: He gathers the lambs in His arms and carries them close to His heart; He gently leads those that have young." ~ Isaiah 40:11

Oh Father allow me to skip like a ram in Your mountains and hills. Let me tell others how You gently lead Your lambs, how You carry us close to Your heart. Savior like a shepherd lead us, much we need Your tender care.

"As the mountains surround Jerusalem, so the LORD surrounds His people both now and forevermore." ~ Psalm 125:2

"How beautiful on the mountains are the feet of those who bring good news, who proclaim peace, who bring good tidings, who proclaim salvation, who say to Zion, 'Your God reigns!'" ~ Isaiah 52:7

Lord surround our home and every aspect of our lives that we may bring glory and honor to Your name. Let me write for Your glory. Allow me this request dear Lord to write so that others may know Your magnificence and to experience and touch Your amazing love. Let my feet be beautiful to You, to proclaim peace, good tidings, and salvation.

"You will go out in joy and be led forth in peace; the mountains and hills will burst into song before you, and all the trees of the field will clap their hands." ~ Isaiah 55:12

Lord, in my quiet time in Illinois you showed me these verses and others. You brought us out of the frozen-north country and brought us forth with joy and peace. Lord, you have showed me through dreams and visions the home in the rolling hills or mountains. Oh Lord how my soul longs to see Your mountains and hills. Please heal my hip Lord that I may dance among Your beauty and my feet may bring the good news to others.

"He who forms the mountains, creates the wind, and reveals His thoughts to man, He who turns dawn to darkness, and treads the high places of the earth—the LORD God Almighty is His name." ~ Amos 4:13

Lord speak for Your servant listens. Let me hear that which You reveal. Oh Father turn my darkness into dawn. Allow me this request, to tread the high places with You, to drink in Your glory, to bathe in Your beauty that I may share with others the hope and the unfailing love that You bestow. Lord I ask for any honor to go to You Lord. Please never let me get puffed up or proud. Take me home Lord before I dishonor You.

"Look, there on the mountains, the feet of one who brings good news, who proclaims peace!" ~ Nahum 1:15

"'Go up into the mountains and bring down timber and build the house, so that I may take pleasure in it and be honored,' says the LORD." ~ Haggai 1:8

Oh sweet Father, let me be one of those who brings good news! Please Father may I go into the mountains and build a house that may bring You pleasure and honor.

"In the last days the mountain of the LORD'S temple will be established as chief among the mountains; it will be raised above the hills, and peoples will stream to it." ~ Micah 4:1

How I long to be with You sweet Father to be one of those that stream into Your temple on Your Holy Mountain! Bring me safely to Your sweet arms. My soul longs with the Psalmist as the deer pants for water. Sweet Jesus thank you for making a way for me to come Home.

Idaho is now our home and the mountains can be seen from our windows. The rivers play in the forest and cross the desert. I've published seven books, my blog has been visited by over 140,000, my Facebook and Twitter feed goes out to thousands to declare the greatness of our God. God has fulfilled my dreams beyond what I could imagine.

Would you be willing to write out your requests to God? Talk with Him. Read His word. God is faithful. The wait may seem long, the journey may be difficult, but God is always faithful.

Thank You, Father for every answered prayer! Thank You Father for everything!

Verses from NIV

~ Called To Harvest ~

My husband and I met Mack and Dottie Kearney in 1995. Mack was our Sunday school teacher, and we were immediately drawn to the couple's heart and passion for God.

With great joy, I bring you Mack's story.

Mack writes, "The year was 1977 and the Lord was doing a new fresh work in my life, bringing me to a place of understanding regarding the Spirit Filled Life and the Crucified Life. Reading missionary biographies, books, and listening to sermons on the subjects, I began to move into this new truth (for me). The Word of God began to be more real and personal. That same year I was invited to go to India and Haiti to preach as a layman and a deacon. Already very comfortable sharing my faith with anyone, this seemed the natural, normal thing for me to do.

"God opened my eyes, and I was now uncomfortable with just throwing money at missions. I knew God had more in mind. I felt Him whetting my appetite for more of Him and the things in His heart. God had been faithful to provide for the expenses of those mission trips, so I was beginning to understand whatever God initiated He would provide.

"I continued to carry this burden for months until one morning in 1978. I told Dottie I was going into our home office, and I didn't want to be disturbed. She asked me how long I would be. I told her I didn't know, but I was going to pray and stay before God until I heard from Him. Later that afternoon, I came out a different man.

"God spoke to me in so many ways. First He dealt with me about the sins in my life. Upon confessing those sins and weeping over them, He gave me a promise from His Word that sealed my heart with His forever. It was from Colossians 3:2, 'Set your mind on things above, not on things on earth.' From that moment, I knew I could trust God to lead me and provide for us wherever He would send us.

"Gospel Harvesters International (GHI) was born, and we are still living out that promise today. We now have a Church planting mission organization with 42 missionaries under our umbrella. Over the last 34 years Gospel Harvesters International has ministered in over 35 different countries throughout the world. This also includes ministries operating in West Africa, India, along with a Bible College and Orphanage in India. God continues to lead and every time we see the cloud in front of us move, we move with Him."

One man touched by our Awesome God to spread the good news. As a result, over 125,000 first time decisions for Christ have been made every year. Wow!

Thank you, Mack and Dottie for your faithful service to our incredible God!

Mack Kearney's story used with his permission

~ Grit To Glory ~

Sand as far as the eye can see, however only the sand which submits to intense heat becomes glass. And that glass shines, reflects, and allows light to pass through.

And in the same way, God wants to refine us to allow His light to shine in our hearts and reflect His love. God's Word reminds us of the blessings of His refinement.

Take the grit of this life, submit it all to God, and let His glory shine through.

"In this you greatly rejoice, though now for a little while you may have had to suffer grief in all kinds of trials. These have come so that your faith—of greater worth than gold, which perishes even though refined by fire—may be proved genuine and may result in praise, glory and honor when Jesus Christ is revealed." ~ 1 Peter 1:6-7 (NIV)

"For You, O God, have proved us; You have tried us as silver is tried, refined, and purified." ~ Psalm 66:10 (AMP)

"And we, who with unveiled faces all reflect the Lord's glory, are being transformed into his likeness with ever-increasing glory, which comes from the Lord, who is the Spirit." ~ 2 Corinthians 3:18 (NIV)

"Let your light so shine before men that they may see your moral excellence and your praiseworthy, noble, and good deeds and recognize and honor and praise and glorify your Father Who is in heaven." ~ Matthew 5:16 (AMP)

"Then will the righteous (those who are upright and in right standing with God) shine forth like the sun in the kingdom of their Father." ~ Matthew 13:43 (AMP)

Heavenly Father thank You that even in the grittiness of life, You refine, purify, transform, and glorify us so we may shine like the sun eternally in Your glorious kingdom.

~ Rocking And Rolling ~

The huge boulder in the middle of the river beckoned. Could I reach the rock without winding up drenched or forty miles downstream?

My sweet hubby watched anxiously on the shore. He stayed in ready mode, prepared to jump in after me in case I took a literal nose dive. His gaze alternated between watching my progress and enjoying the eagles tending to their babies in a nest high above the river.

The water was cool and amazingly clear. I had no idea if the depth was two feet or twenty. I finally found a route by walking up river then maneuvering down through shallow sections.

Finally safe on the boulder, I sat mesmerized. The river hit with force against the rock face, but behind remained a tranquil, deep pool.

Once situated, I dangled one foot into the wild water and the other into the calm. The moment was amazing. I asked God to burn that experience into my mind so I would never forget the feeling of one foot thrashing around and the other lazily bobbing in peaceful water.

The old hymn came to mind, "On Christ the solid rock I stand." Although I didn't dare try to stand, I remained safe and immovable.

I love the visual reminder that no matter what comes against us we are eternally secure in our God The rock of all ages.

Happy contented sigh

"God is bedrock under my feet, the castle in which I live, my rescuing knight. My God—the high crag where I run for dear life, hiding behind the boulders, safe in the granite hideout; my mountaintop refuge, he saves me from ruthless men. The Lord is my rock, my protection, my Savior. My God is my rock. I can run to him for safety. He is my shield and my saving strength, my defender." ~ 2 Samuel 22:3 (MSG), Psalm 18:2 (NCV)

~ Honor ~

"I will honor those who honor me." ~ 1 Samuel 2:30 (NLT)

"God may allow the wicked to win worldly honors; but the dignity which He Himself gives, even glory, honor, and immortality, He reserves for those who by holy obedience take care to honor Him." ~ C. H. Spurgeon

I wonder how different life would be if we as Christians truly looked to honor God over the desire to honor ourselves.

Which will you choose? Fleeting or eternal honor?

Heavenly Father, life here is so temporary. There is no award or honor the world can bestow that will last for eternity. However in honoring You, comes the blessing of a deeper, fuller ever-lasting, loving relationship with You. Praising You forever, for You are worthy of all honor, glory, and praise!

~ Breathless ~

"The queen of Sheba heard of Solomon's reputation and came to Jerusalem to put his reputation to the test, asking all the tough questions. She made a showy entrance—an impressive retinue of attendants and camels loaded with perfume and much gold and precious stones. She emptied her heart to Solomon, talking over everything she cared about.

"And Solomon answered everything she put to him—nothing stumped him.

"When the queen of Sheba experienced for herself Solomon's wisdom and saw with her own eyes the palace he had built, the meals that were served, the impressive array of court officials, the sharply dressed waiters, the cupbearers, and then the elaborate worship extravagant with Whole-Burnt-Offerings at The Temple of God, **it all took her breath away**." ~ 2 Chronicles 9:2-4 MSG

I read this passage and wondered…

When others see God is in us, and see what God has done in our lives, **will they come seeking Him, and leave breathless in wonder**?

Heavenly Father, help me to live in such a way, speak in such a way, stay so close to You, that others are drawn to You and left breathless in Your loving wonder!

~ Tummy Trauma, Prayers, And Police ~

During my battle with Lyme disease, I encountered major stomach issues. After trying a bevy of over-the-counter remedies without results, the doctor was called. Forty-five minutes after an office visit I was sent to the Emergency room for possible surgery.

Family, friends, and cyber-buddies rallied their prayers. Our teenage son remained at home with several friends. My husband waited with me as doctors and nurses took blood, x-ray's, and hooked up an IV. Fortunately several hours later I was released with three prescriptions and without the need for surgery.

After a trip to the pharmacy, we returned to our neighborhood and followed a police cruiser down our street. The officer slowed down and seemed to be making a u-turn in our cul-de-sac.

We parked our car in the garage, and as we walked inside the house, the doorbell rang. A police officer stood outside. Not sure what to expect, we opened the door.

My son and his friends gathered at the top of the stairs.

The police officer explained he had received a disturbing the peace call reporting loud music. But then with a smile, went on to clarify the report came from our house.

Yes, you read that right. Our son and his friends had called.

We chuckled wondering if this was the first time in history teenagers reported loud music. The officer explained the overly loud sounds came from a concert at a nearby park.

Everyone thanked the policeman, and the guys happily thumped back upstairs. My tummy problems quieted down, as did the neighborhood.

Don't you love that no matter what our complaint or problem, we have a God who is always ready to respond. All you need to do is call.

"I call to you in times of trouble, because you will answer me." ~ Psalm 86:7 (NCV)

~ My Self Needs You ~

I want to die to self so I may live fully in Christ. Heavenly Father my self needs You.

I want the **A-Z** of me to be dead to me to live fully in Christ.

Replace my self-**A**wareness to be aware of only You.

I want to replace any self-**B**elief with God-belief.

Remind my self-**C**ondemnation of Romans 8:1, there is no condemnation for those in Christ Jesus.

Make Your reality and truth over any self-**D**elusions.

Let my self-**E**steem come from You and not my own self-**F**ocus.

Replace my self-**G**ratification with the deeper gratification of serving You.

When self-**H**ate rears its ugly head, remind me of Your unfailing love.

I want to get away from any self-**I**nfatuation, self-indulgence, and self-**J**ustification.

Help me base any self-**K**nowledge through the knowledge of You.

When self-**L**oathing slithers in, remind me I am lovingly, fearfully, and wonderfully made by You.

Replace any self-**M**indedness with a mind to focus squarely on You.

Stop any negative self-**N**arrative with the truth found in the narrative of Your Word.

Replace my self-**O**bsession by the glorious obsession of You.

Remind my self-**P**ity of every blessing which You so freely bestow.

When self-**Q**uestioning comes questioning, help me remember all answers are found in You.

Cleanse out any self-**R**ighteous, **S**elf-reliance, self-serving, self-**T**houghts, self-**U**nderstanding, that seek to self-validate, or self-**V**indicate.

Take my self-**W**ill and bend it to Your will.

I don't want to be self-**X**eroxing unless I'm xeroxing me in You.

Help my self-**Y**akking replaced with speaking of You and praising You.

Heavenly Father, every part of my self-**Z**one, the **A-Z** of me commits myself to You.

~ Soul Riches ~

Society is consumed with consumerism and passionate about the pursuit of wealth. We forget anything this world offers is only temporary. The only possessions that will remain involve our souls.

It's easy to think wealth will solve all our problems. But money doesn't save. Riches might buy medical care, but can't provide soul-healing. Monetary wealth might make us feel more secure, but can't provide eternal security.

At birth, I arrived with nothing -- no clothes, no belongings, and no speech other than a cry. Based on what I had when I arrived, much has been given. No matter how little I posses, my riches are beyond measure. And when death comes, I can take nothing but the one thing that matters the most—an eternal relationship with Jesus Christ, my Savior.

Nothing is greater than knowing Christ Jesus as Lord, because everything else perishes, spoils or fades. So don't put your hope in wealth, which is uncertain and temporary, put your hope in God who richly provides us everything for our enjoyment. For an inheritance in Christ results in incorruptible eternal riches. Are you eternally soul rich?

Heavenly Father thank You for the rich treasure of Your forgiveness, grace, and mercy. Help me to remember I am eternally rich in Your love.

~ Salvation Shoes ~

Sunday school teacher, Edward Kimball decided the time had finally come to speak to his wayward pupil, Dwight. For eleven months Dwight had attended Kimball's church, but still hadn't come to terms with Christianity.

Kimball arrived at the shoe store where Dwight worked. Not wanting to embarrass him by witnessing in front of the other clerks, Kimball almost turned around and left. Instead, he decided to "make a dash for it and have it over at once."

Finding the young man in the back of the store, Kimball looked Dwight in the eyes and asked him to come to Christ who loved him and who wanted his love. On that day, Saturday, April 21, 1855, Dwight L. Moody prayed to receive Christ.

A changed man, D. L. Moody became an evangelist, spreading the Good News about Christ throughout the world. During Moody's lifetime, he founded several churches and institutions including Moody Church and Moody Bible Institute in Chicago. And the estimates of those who heard the gospel through Dwight Moody are estimated at no less than a hundred million people. Wow!

One Sunday school teacher, one shoe clerk, and one Awesome God!

"How beautiful on the mountains are the feet of the messenger who brings good news, the good news of peace and salvation, the news that the God of Israel reigns!" ~ Isaiah 52:7 (NLT)

~ Words Of Love ~

On a warm Texas evening in June, our church congregation met in our sanctuary undergoing renovation. The pews and carpet had been removed exposing the bare concrete. We prayed and sang praises to dedicate the renewing of the sanctuary. We sang "Holy, Holy, Holy, Lord God Almighty", the sound reverberating off the bare walls and floor. Truly, the Lord was present.

Those who had been charter members and our earliest elders were given twelve stones as a memorial (Joshua 3-4) to place in the soon-to-be renewed building. The rest of the congregation knelt on the bare floor. And with markers, pens, or pencils, we wrote scriptures, love notes to God, or the names of those who were being lifted up for salvation.

How amazing and wonderful to watch young and old on their knees writing scripture. How precious to see little ones leaving sweet phrases. We were truly standing on the promises of God! Tiny hands had written their verses with letters misspelled or reversed, pictures of crosses, hearts and words of love. One little one wrote "I Love Gob" in wobbly handwriting. You could almost feel the angels hovering overhead watching, reading, and delighting in God's children praising Him.

The following Monday, workers returned to finish the renovation. Every piece of tile, every piece of carpeting and wood placed over those words were viewed by workers. Each word watering, budding, prospering and accomplishing God's will.

"For as the rain comes down, and the snow from heaven, and do not return there, but water the earth, and make it bring forth and bud, that it may give seed to the sower and bread to the eater, so shall My word be that goes forth from My mouth; It shall not return to Me void, but it shall accomplish what I please, and it shall prosper in the thing for which I sent it." ~ Isaiah 55:10-11 (NKJV)

God's word never returns void, and when we speak and write His words, mighty things are accomplished in lives for eternity!

Heavenly Father help me to remember Your words, speak Your words, and write Your words, for Your words hold all the power of heaven and earth!

~ A Father's Love ~

Even if you didn't have a loving earthly father, your Father in Heaven loves you more than you can imagine. God gave me such a beautiful visual while I waited at an airport.

A dad ran to his wife and two little girls. They all embraced, and then the dad did something that melted my heart. The father hugged each little girl, and then bent down to look at each one intently and individually. As one little girl talked, his loving gaze never left her face. Then he turned to the other, and listened as she shared.

God is your loving heavenly Father. And when you talk to Him, He leans down from heaven to intently listen to His beloved child. He loves you and is so glad you are His.

Heavenly Father how amazing that You love me. Help me to accept Your love and understand that You are always waiting and watching for when I come home, and when I call. I love You, Father.

~ Peace Like A River ~

Horatio Spafford was a successful attorney in Chicago, active in church, and blessed with a wife and four daughters. A series of calamities began when the great Chicago fire of 1871 wiped out his families extensive real estate investments. Even through the tough times Spafford held firm to his belief and faith in God. Spafford was a friend and supporter of the great evangelist D.L. Moody. When Moody began a campaign in Great Britain; Spafford planned to join them to assist. Seeing this as a wonderful opportunity for the whole family, passage was booked on the *S.S. Ville du Harve* in November of 1873.

Before he could leave, he was detained by urgent business. He sent his family ahead and planned to join them as soon as possible. Unfortunately the ship carrying his wife and daughters was struck by an English vessel and sank in twelve minutes. Two hundred and twenty six people drowned, including his four daughters. Only his wife miraculously survived.

Heartbroken, Spafford boarded another ship to meet his bereaved wife. Upon reaching the approximate sight of the shipwreck, he stood on the deck of his ship. Sensing God's presence and unexplained peace, he wrote these words. "When peace like a river, attendeth my way, when sorrows like sea billows roll—whatever my lot, Thou hast taught me to say, it is well with my soul."

How can one write, "It is well with my soul", when tragedy has just struck? Only through God. Only God can make us "well with our soul" in the midst of tragedy and turmoil.

Peace is found through a soul perspective, looking beyond today to the forever. When God is our focus, our direction, and our love, there is nothing on earth that can shake, or remove our eternal stability.

It is well with my soul because … In peace I lie down and sleep, For You alone, O LORD, makes me dwell in safety (Psalm 4:8).

It is well with my soul because even when doors seem locked Jesus comes and says, "Peace to you!" (John 20:26)

It is well with my soul because the fruit of righteousness is peace; the effect of righteousness is quietness and confidence forever (Isaiah 32:17).

It is well with my soul because You, Lord, give true peace to those who depend on You, because they trust You (Isaiah 26:3)

It is well with my soul because the name of the LORD is a strong tower; the righteous run into it and are safe (Proverbs 18:10).

It is well with my soul because Jesus promises that in Him we have peace. In the world we have tribulation, but we can take courage; because He has overcome the world (John 16:33)

Heavenly Father thank You that no matter what difficulties are suffering comes, that in You we can always find peace.

"Therefore, having been justified by faith, we have peace with God through our Lord Jesus Christ" ~ Romans 5:1 (NKJV)

~ To Love Much ~

How do you view your forgiveness? Do you compare your sins to others, maximizing theirs and minimizing yours?

Do you rejoice in your forgiveness because your sins have been many? Or is your forgiveness "no big deal" since you've been a "pretty good" person?

Did you realize only one sin would keep you from a Holy God? Just one.

Just. One. Sin.

How much do you love God for His mercy and grace?

For the sacrifice Jesus made for you, do you love much?

"And there was a woman in the city who was a sinner; and when she learned that He was reclining at the table in the Pharisee's house, she brought an alabaster vial of perfume, and standing behind Him at His feet, weeping, she began to wet His feet with her tears, and kept wiping them with the hair of her head, and kissing His feet and anointing them with the perfume.

"Now when the Pharisee who had invited Him saw this, he said to himself, 'If this man were a prophet He would know who and what sort of person this woman is who is touching Him, that she is a sinner.'"

"And Jesus answered him, 'Simon, I have something to say to you.' And he replied, 'Say it, Teacher.' 'A moneylender had two debtors: one owed five hundred denarii, and the other fifty. When they were unable to repay, he graciously forgave them both. So which of them will love him more?'

"Simon answered and said, 'I suppose the one whom he forgave more.'

"And He said to him, 'You have judged correctly.' Turning toward the woman, He said to Simon, 'Do you see this woman? I entered your house; you gave Me no water for My feet, but she has wet My feet with her tears and wiped them with her hair. You gave Me no kiss; but she, since the time I came in, has not ceased to kiss My feet. You did not anoint My head with oil, but she anointed My feet with perfume. For this reason I say to you, her sins, which are many, have been forgiven, for **she loved much; but he who is forgiven little, loves little.'"** Luke 7:37-47 (NASB)

~ Bless Them ~

Jesus said to "Bless those who curse you." How can we do this? How is this possible? Here are some ideas.

For those who don't know God. Father, bless them with open hearts to Your salvation. Bless them with open eyes to see You.

For those who make your work miserable. Father, bless them with a new job far, far away. :)

For those who make your life miserable. Bless them with Your love, Father.

For those who are evil. Father, bless them with the knowledge of good and evil. Bless them to know right from wrong. Bless them to see Your truth and turn from their wicked ways.

For those who are hard-hearted. Father, bless them with a sensitive heart.

For the ones who are wayward. Father, bless them to see life the way You desire and the blessings of living in Your love.

For those who you know, who trouble you, who mock you, who make fun of you, who have left you … how can you bless them?

"Bless those who curse you. Pray for those who hurt you." ~ Luke 6:28 (NLT)

~ Faith In Action ~

I woke early this morning with this thought, "The faith fails because, the faith sits." And as I pondered that statement, I realized that true faith is faith in action. It is faith to step out of the boat in the middle of storms. Faith to do what the world deems impossible, yet knowing that nothing is impossible with God.

And I wondered if we aren't getting anything done for God's Kingdom, because we aren't kingdom minded. We aren't living out our faith in action.

Faith in action is the eighty year old woman who uses six sewing machines to make baby clothes for the poor.

Faith in action is the seventy-six year old woman who is selling everything to move to Haiti and love on orphan children.

Faith in action is the women who makes side pockets for those who have wheelchairs--pockets to carry books, glasses, medications or other necessities.

Faith in action is the sixty-five people who support a ministry that has preached to millions throughout the world.

Faith in action is the children who save their allowance to share with others.

Faith in action is the young people who work on weekends to help stock food banks.

Faith in action is those who have little energy, but pray mighty prayers.

Faith in action is through those who believe God's promises, and step out in faith knowing that God always keeps His promises.

Is your faith not only active, but activated? Are you living faith in action?

"It is impossible to please God without faith. Anyone who wants to come to him must believe that God exists and that he rewards those who sincerely seek him." ~ Hebrews 11:6 (NLT)

"Faith by itself isn't enough. Unless it produces good deeds, it is dead and useless. Now someone may argue, 'Some people have faith; others have good deeds.' But I say, 'How can you show me your faith if you don't have good deeds? I will show you my faith by my good deeds.' You say you have faith, for you believe that there is one God. Good for you! Even the demons believe this, and they tremble in terror. How foolish! Can't you see that faith without good deeds is useless?" ~ James 2:17-19 (NLT)

"'You don't have enough faith,' Jesus told them. 'I tell you the truth, if you had faith even as small as a mustard seed, you could say to this mountain, 'Move from here to there,' and it would move. Nothing would be impossible. And if God cares so wonderfully for wildflowers that are here today and thrown into the fire tomorrow, he will certainly care for you. Why do you have so little faith? I tell you the truth, anyone who believes in me will do the same works I have done, and even greater works, because I am going to be with the Father." ~ Matthew 17:20, Matthew 6:30, John 14:12 (NLT)

"But realize this, that in the last days difficult times will come. For men will be lovers of self, lovers of money, boastful, arrogant, revilers, disobedient to parents, ungrateful, unholy, unloving, irreconcilable, malicious gossips, without self-control, brutal, haters of good, treacherous, reckless, conceited, lovers of pleasure rather than lovers of God, holding to a form of godliness, although they have denied its power. Avoid such men as these." ~ 2 Timothy 3:1-5 (NASB)

"And so he did only a few miracles there because of their unbelief." ~ Matthew 13:58 (NLT)

Heavenly Father help me to put my faith in action and to never deny the power You possess. Help me to step out in faith, never blocking what You want to accomplish, believing completely in who You are and the amazing things You do.

~ Don't Miss The Glory ~

How often do we miss seeing God's glory? Do we pass him by as we hurry to an appointment? Do we forget to walk as Jesus walked leaving glory, hallelujah footprints?

I see God's glory on the pages of His word. I see His glory in the faces of those at church and Bible study. I saw His glory as I shopped at the grocery store. A little girl visited with a handicapped man. God was in that moment as they talked and laughed. Sweet fellowship. Sweet interaction. And in my spirit The voice whispered, *"Did I not tell you that if you believed you would see the glory of God?"**

2000 years ago a baby was born and laid in a manger. But this baby wasn't ordinary; He was the only begotten Son of God. Jesus Christ grew into a man leaving footprints straight to the cross where he died. But three days later, death couldn't contain His glory and He arose to grant us new life. There is nothing more glorious than our Savior. Let's walk as Jesus walked leaving glory, hallelujah footprints.

Watch for how God works and whispers, and how He reveals Himself. O that our eyes would remain open to see and our spirits open to believe. Watch and believe, dear friends. And you too, will see God's glory.

"Jesus said to her, 'Did I not tell you and promise you that if you would believe and rely on Me, you would see the glory of God?" ~ John 11:40 (AMP)

~ Broken Into Beautiful ~

I "met" Gwen Smith online several years ago when I asked her permission to post the lyrics to her wonderful song, "Broken into Beautiful." I loved the song, but then I read her amazing testimony. We truly have a God who can take and turn anyone's broken life into a thing of beauty. Gwen Smith is living proof.

With her permission, below is her story in her own words…

"I remember the phone call to my college boyfriend. Through sobs, I managed to tell him I was pregnant. There was a long pause on the other end of the phone … and then came the speed round of questions and comments: 'What are we going to do? Do you think we should get married? Oh, my gosh … Oh, my gosh…what are we going to do? Do you want to have this baby? What are we going to do? What about volleyball? What will your parents say? What will my parents say? Oh, my gosh!'

"Like trapped animals, we were frantically looking for a way out. Then we made our decision. We would take care of it. It wasn't time for us to have a baby yet. God wasn't consulted. He wasn't invited into our decision. My boyfriend and I hid from God and did what we considered to be our only option. We made a plan. My boyfriend would pick me up and take me to a clinic I read about in the yellow pages.

"When the day came, we drove in icy silence. I was Fort Knox. No one was going to break through the emotional walls I had constructed for protection. You see there was never a moment I believed having an abortion was the right thing to do. I only stubbornly and naively believed my choice was the only ladder to grab out of the horrible pit I had dug for myself.

"I was wrong. Dead wrong. There, in the sterile room of that stale clinic, I used an alias. I wasn't Gwen. My charts did not say that I was Gwen, the girl who was raised by good parents, the girl who was raised in the Word of God to know right from wrong. The counselor I had met with said using my name could have made me feel uncomfortable with the 'harmless and legal procedure' I was having done that day. Nobody else needed to know. I was anonymous.

"It was my secret. A secret of chains that bound me in silence for the ensuing fifteen years – a secret kept because I mistakenly assumed no one else could handle the ugly truth of my sinfulness with grace and forgiveness. I was a Christian girl. Christians don't get pregnant when they aren't married, and Christians don't have abortions, right? It was all too scandalous, and I was crazy afraid of the consequences.

"Most of that gloomy, cold January day was a blur. Though the clinic was lit with bright fluorescent lights, the flame of dignity and hope in my heart had grown dim. I blocked out all the voices in my head as they contested what I was doing. I was desperate and scared.

"For weeks following my abortion, I went through each day under a dark cloud of despair. I couldn't reconcile what I had done with who I was, and who I was supposed to be. My heart was broken. I felt hopeless and was horribly ashamed. I hated what I had done, and I hated myself for doing it. I was responsible for the death of my baby. It was my fault. I knew it, and it haunted me.

"Voices of accusation used to scream in my head. They shouted things like: Murderer! Baby killer! Hypocrite! You can never tell a soul about this! Condemnation kept me shackled. Without realizing it, I was a captive to my own acceptance of those words. I was guilty. A wretch. No excuses. My heart was paralyzed by death. Words just can't express the depth of anguish my soul experienced.

"The dark days turned into weeks, which turned into months. Although I could turn on the fake charm like water from a faucet...oh, how my plastic smile served me well in those days...I was dying inside! At night, my pillow soaked up rivers of tears. I would lie awake, wondering if my baby was a boy or girl, or if my baby had felt any pain as she was being sucked from my body.

"I wept. I wept for both my baby and for myself. It was necessary. It felt right to cry. And though the tears helped my soul grieve, none were as healing as the ones I cried to Jesus when I finally turned back to Him. Like Peter after the rooster crowed, I wept bitterly at the feet of Jesus in raw repentance. Then, as the psalmist did, I 'waited patiently for the LORD; He turned to me and heard my cry. He lifted me out of the slimy pit, out of the mud and mire; He set my feet on a rock and gave me a firm place to stand. He put a new song in my mouth, a hymn of praise to our God' (Psalm 40:1-3).

"Although I didn't deserve His mercy, Jesus forgave me. My forgiveness was immediate and complete, but the healing took time. He gave me a new song. Hallelujah! I've been forgiven and transformed by the unconditional love of God. I was dead in my sins, but am now alive in Christ! I am free and it is my privilege to encourage you towards that same freedom in Christ. God longs for you to experience His perfect healing and hope too – no matter what you've done, no matter where you've been, no matter what has left you broken.

"There is no condemnation for those in Christ. While the enemy loves to cast false guilt, our Lord loves to extend grace and forgiveness, which is the remedy that restores all your broken pieces. Don't hold onto those pieces. Don't hide them behind a plastic smile. Bring them into the light, lay them at the feet of Jesus, and let go. Allow your wounds to be healed today."

Today Gwen Smith is a gifted worship leader, songwriter, speaker, and author with a passion for others to experience a deeper relationship with God. She is living proof past failures do not disqualify anyone from service in the Kingdom of God. Through her powerful testimony, disarming humor, Scripture teaching, and Christ-centered music, she invites each individual to experience the unconditional love of Jesus.

Gwen has been featured on many television and radio shows. She is also the cofounder and worship leader of Girlfriends in God, a conference and devotional ministry, and is a contributing writer for the Girlfriends in God daily e-devotions delivered to 500,000+ women subscribers each weekday. She is the author of, *Broken into Beautiful* and contributing author of, *Trusting God: A Girlfriends in God Faith Adventure*.

Gwen encourages women to experience God's forgiveness and allow God's grace and healing to work in their lives transforming their brokenness into His beauty.

Gwen Smith, one broken woman transformed and beautifully restored by our Awesome God!

You can hear more of her testimony on Living Joyfully Free Radio. Please visit Gwen on her website, www.GwenSmith.net and www.GirlfriendsInGod.com

Used by Permission of Gwen Smith and Harvest House Publishers.
Taken from: BROKEN INTO BEAUTIFUL
Copyright © 2008 by Gwen Smith
Published by Harvest House Publishers
Eugene, Oregon 97402
www.harvesthousepublishers.com Used by Permission.

~ Buffaloe Herd Travel Log ~

April 2009, the Buffaloe herd packed the van to the hilt and began the journey from Texas to Boise, Idaho. God protected and guided us through sixty mile-an-hour winds, dust storms, tornado warnings, and fires in Oklahoma which resulted in a shutdown of the interstate and an hour long line of traffic through the back roads.

The verse in Isaiah came to mind... "When you pass through the waters, I will be with you; and when you pass through the rivers, they will not sweep over you. When you walk through the fire, you will not be burned; the flames will not set you ablaze." ~ Isaiah 43:2 NIV

We stopped in Kansas when the snow rain/snow/sleet drove us inside. Our travels restarted early the next morning where we crossed several million, gazillion miles of prairie lands. That night, we stopped in the Wyoming Mountains and rested our weary hoofs. During our travels, we saw Bison, antelope, deer, and elk (oh, give me a home where the Buffaloe roam and the deer and the antelope play). Sorry, couldn't resist. :)

Weaving through the mountains, we felt like kids in a candy store oohing and aahing over God's beautiful creations.

Seventeen hundred and twenty eight (1728!) miles later we arrived safely in Boise. It was interesting along our journey how God provided our every need – including much needed rest stops for troubled tummies.

We settled in a temporary apartment. While my hubby went to his new job, sweet son and I went to the high school in the district where we had planned on buying a house. Even though our son was in the middle of his junior year, he was excited to relocate.

Before we arrived, we had verified that our apartment was in the same district so there wouldn't be any problems. However when we went to register, the school wouldn't let us enroll. He would need to attend another one.

As we stood in the hallway wondering what was happening. A teacher walked by and mentioned he was going to the other high school and would guide us to the location. We visited for a few minutes and learned he attended a church we had considered. We were so grateful God had the man appear at "just the right time" to help us find our way to the school and to his church. Our son accepted the change in stride knowing that God had something neat planned during the remaining six weeks of his junior year.

Even though we stayed in our "temporary" apartment another ten months as we waited for our Texas house to sell, God continued to provide for our every need. Our prayer all along was that God would not send us anywhere that He didn't want us to go. And we felt His presence every step of the way.

It's amazing knowing that God brought us to Idaho – for us and for others. God never does things that are only for us, there will always be a ripple effect in His kingdom. We learn and grow through each new experience and the people God puts in our path. And hopefully we help others learn and grow. What incredible peace knowing God guides our every step, and His way will always be best.

If God is moving you whether physically or spiritually, don't resist. His plans are always the best and always lead to new adventures.

"For I know the plans I have for you,' declares the LORD, 'plans to prosper you and not to harm you, plans to give you hope and a future.'" ~ Jeremiah 29:11 (NIV)

~ Are You Mad? ~

Are you mad at God?

Tell Him.
He's a BIG God. He already knows you are mad.
Tell Him how you feel. God wants the truth and when we think we are hiding how we feel, the only one we are deceiving is ourselves.

Tell God exactly how you feel. Talk to Him. He is waiting.

As you talk, as you tell the truth about how you hurt, how you've been wronged, or the things that are unfair, it cleanses out the wounds.

Talk to Him. Let Him hear what is on your heart -- the good, the bad, and the ugly.

Talk to Him. And as you talk, the truth will set you free.

"For God is Spirit, so those who worship him must worship in spirit and in truth. And you will know the truth, and the truth will set you free." ~ John 4:24, John 8:32 (NLT)

~ Red Alert! ~

When our Texas house was on the market and officially listed on the Realtor sites, Buffaloeville needed to be in tip-top shape and ready to show at a moment's notice. One evening, sweet hubby and I propped our feet up in the recliners and turned on the television while our son played an online game. Our peace and quiet was shattered when a phone call alerted us that a Realtor was on the way.

Red alert!

The family fanned out to check each room, shut down electronics, and make sure everything was ready. We grabbed the dog, jumped into the Buffaloemobile, and sped into the night. Well we actually crept down the street in the family van, hoping to see whoever was coming to view our home.

That night's adventure is a good reminder to always be ready. The same is true for our spiritual lives. Paul urged Timothy to be prepared in season and out of season (2 Timothy 4:2). And if I don't keep my spiritual house in order, I can't be ready for whatever God has planned in my life.

I love having a clean house, and I want to keep a clean heart—both take work. Ah, but the benefits are great. Anyone could drop by my house, and I'd be proud to give them a tour. Spiritually, if I stay in God's word and keep my mind focused on Him, I'm more prepared to be open to His leading.

You never know when the call may come.

Are you ready?

~ *Thankful* ~

I'm overwhelmingly, abundantly blessed by those who I have met throughout my life. Unique personalities, views, and thoughts of each person amazes me.

I'm thankful for family, friends, writer buddies, cyber-friends, and those who I only know through a quick e-mail or social site connection. I'm thankful for what each one has taught me and for the glimpses of their lives.

The hug, the pat on the arm, the e-mail note, the phone call, the smile, through each person and their individual personalities, I have seen more of God.

I have so much to be thankful for. I'm thankful first and foremost for a loving God who sent His Son to make a way for us to be in Heaven. I'm so grateful for each of you. Thank you for taking the time to read this book—I'm honored. You bless my day.

Have you ever heard a little child pray? They thank God for the caterpillars, the birds, the trees, for tickles, mud, sunshine, puppies, kittens, and the list continues. Maybe that's why Jesus tells us to become like children. If we looked at life as an innocent child, wouldn't we have lots more fun?

What if?

What if today we could only keep that for which we were thankful? At the end of the day, what would remain?

Dear Heavenly Father, thank You! Thank You for all Your wonderful blessings. Thank You, Thank You, Thank You! Thank You for every person who reads this book. Father, I lift each one of them up to You. Meet them at their every point of need. Where there is pain, bring comfort. Where there is illness, I pray for healing. For those that are weak, grant them Your strength.

And for those who are lonely, help them feel Your sweet, loving presence. I love You so much Father!

Thank You Jesus for coming to earth to save us. Holy Spirit breathe God's words into me that I may share with others the wonders of God and His love. I'm so thankful! My heart might burst.

I thankfully ask these things in the precious Name of Your Son, Jesus Christ, Amen.

~ No Other Love ~

God is love.
And love (God) gives love.
The only love we can depend on is God's love.
The only love we should depend on is God's love.

If we are exhausted from loving, it's because we're trying to love in our own power.

We can love freely with God's love because God gives His love freely, unending, unlimited, limitless, and inexhaustible.
Because God is love.

God's love flowed through the blood of Jesus to bring love.

Love died to bring love to a dying world.
Love rose from the dead to love us into new life.
There is no other love greater.

Greater love has no one than this, that someone lay down his life for his friends. For God so loved the world, that He gave his only Son, that whoever believes in Him should not perish but have eternal life. (John 15:13, John 3:16-17)

~ Living In Enemy Territory ~

Those of us who belong to Christ are strangers, aliens, and peculiar people. We forget we aren't of this world. Christians are on mission, secret agents, sent to enemy territory to help set captives free. We know where freedom is found, and we can share The Good News.

Why have we lost our bravery? Those of us who are invincible, why aren't we brave? Why do we wilt and run at the first sign of trouble or during disappointment or heartache? Why aren't we standing firm when difficulties come?

Jesus said we will have trouble, but He has overcome the world. Oh that we would be brave as we remember, as we know, we have eternal hope. Oh that we would be brave to walk on this dusty earth, knowing our true homes are prepared for eternity, an eternity full of unending joy and peace.

Be brave, stand firm on the solid rock. **Be brave**, God's might and power are greater than anything in our out of this world. **Be brave**, and watch what God will do through you. **Live brave** while living in enemy territory, and **tell others of the freedom found in Christ, so they too can be brave**.

"So be strong and courageous! Do not be afraid and do not panic before them. For the LORD your God will personally go ahead of you. He will neither fail you nor abandon you." ~ Deuteronomy 31:6 (NLT)

~ Think Bigger ~

Think bigger. Whatever you think you can achieve, whatever you think you can overcome, add to it infinitely to get to God sized. Bigger, much bigger, much, much, Much Bigger!

God who created the Heavens and earth, who calms the seas, drives out demons, takes a handful of bread and fish and feeds thousands, that same God will do exceedingly more than you can ever ask or imagine.

Whatever you face, whatever mountains loom ahead, God is bigger. God has more planned; more excitement and more joy for the journey. God doesn't create us only to live, but to abundant, free-flowing, everlasting life!

With God there is always more than we can imagine –more grace, more power, more love, more strength, and more possibilities in the impossibilities of life.

With God, not just some, not just a little, but much, much BIGGER things are planned for here and for eternity.

For with God ALL things are possible.

Think BIGGER with God and live joyfully free!

~ About The Author ~

Lisa Buffaloe is a writer, speaker, founder and radio host for Living Joyfully Free Radio, happily-married wife, and mom. Lisa's past experiences—molestation by a baby-sitter, assault, rape by a doctor, divorce, being stalked, cancer, death of loved ones, seven surgeries, and eleven years of chronic illness from Lyme Disease—bless her with a backdrop to share God's amazing love. God's love is unending and through Jesus Christ we find healing, restoration, and renewal.

Lisa is the author of *Nadia's Hope, Prodigal Nights, Living Joyfully Free Devotional Volumes 1 and 2, Grace for the Char-Baked, No Wound Too Deep For The Deep Love Of Christ*, and *Unfailing Treasures Devotional*.

Please visit Lisa at…
www.lisabuffaloe.com
www.livingjoyfullyfree.com
www.Facebook.com/lisabuffaloe
www.Twitter.com/lisabuffaloe

Additional Books By Lisa Buffaloe

Living Joyfully Free Devotional, Volume 1

Finding Freedom, Hope and Joy ~

Living joyfully free is falling back into God's arms and releasing your worries, problems, concerns, and fears. Living joyfully free doesn't mean you won't have trouble or problems; it is allowing God to take full control—trusting and believing He has your best interest at heart.

This isn't a regular devotion book. Each page is a stepping stone, a place to pause and ponder, a field to run through, a mountain to climb, a river to splash and play in God's Living water. Let's have a picnic with The Bread of Life and spend time Son-kissed by God's Son.

God invites you to live joyfully free. Explore how you can start today.

Nadia's Hope
2010 Women of Faith Writing Contest finalist
**The Nightmares continue. Memories won't heal.
Nadia must make a choice.**

Nadia Minsky fled Israel to escape her past, but she can't outrun her nightmares. The throbbing scars along her hip and stomach are cruel reminders of shattered dreams. Even though surgeons mended her body, her spirit still bleeds. Friends claim only God can heal her. For Nadia, trusting a God who allowed her to suffer is inconceivable.

Can close friends, a wild roommate, and a handsome medical student, help Nadia learn to trust? Or will she chose to allow her past to forever cripple her future?

Prodigal Nights
2011 Women of Faith Writing Contest finalist
For two returning prodigals will the challenge to live "good" withstand the allure to be bad?

After a nasty divorce, Bethany Davis returned to college and lived up to the low standards set by gossips. Her dad's stroke has now brought her home, and Bethany finds herself in a dilemma--how can she get beyond her past, learn to trust again, and live a "good" life?

Bethany's father's involvement in the defense industry adds excitement to her expectation of a boring life back home. However, bodyguards, stalkers, and international secrets are the least of her problems--opening her heart to trust again is a totally different matter. And the mutual attraction with her new team leader, Jason Ross, spells the possibility of big-time heart trouble.

Jason's days of wild living are over, and he's determined to prove to himself and God that he's on the right path. When Bethany steps into his office, he sees the girl of his dreams, but is she God's gift or Satan's temptress?

Grace for the Char-Baked (Novella)

With "Char" as a nickname, Charlotte Wilson's cooking skills are more incendiary than culinary. Charlotte is the last person on earth who should run a bake sale. But when her plans of running in a charity marathon are sidelined by a broken foot, her old flame's suggestion becomes a challenge amidst her friend's simmering doubts.

Luke Hammond has spent the last five years studying and preparing to travel overseas as a medical missionary. When his high school sweetheart unexpectedly comes back in his life, Luke wrestles with what he feels God calling him to be and what he wants to do. His reappearance rekindles an attraction that could char Luke and Charlotte's heart or cook up the perfect romance.

No Wound Too Deep For The Deep Love of Christ

The enemy wants you to believe your wounds are incurable and your past is unredeemable; that your pain, your sin, and your experiences are too far from God's healing touch. The past cannot be erased, but we can take every wound to the Great Physician – God.

God loves you just as you are – wounded, battered, bruised. God loves you – your past and the hidden things no one knows. God loves you – your jagged scars that carved valleys in your soul. God loves you – and no one and nothing can keep Him from you. No person. No power on earth. No memory. No flashback. No sin. No thought. No action. Nothing can stop God from offering His healing and His everlasting, unfailing love.

The One who made you, the One who loves you with an unfailing love, He is The One who wants to heal you and The One who can heal you.

No Wound Too Deep gently beckons you to experience the deep, healing love of God.

Unfailing Treasures Devotional

Treasure is sought after, fought over, and pursued to the ends of the earth. Yet no matter how much wealth is gained, nothing is safe from thieves, decay, or the fluctuating world economy. And not one penny can be taken beyond the grave.

However there is an amazing offer for unfailing treasures, secure, and transportable beyond space and time. Satisfaction, love, joy, peace, comfort, and everything your soul craves, is offered for free. An incredible treasure room filled with unfailing, heavenly treasures waits for all.

You Can Take It With You.

An unfailing treasure in heaven, where no thief comes near nor moth destroys. ~ Luke 12:33

Living Joyfully Free
Volume 2

Lisa Buffaloe

Made in the USA
San Bernardino, CA
04 February 2017